FOLKTALES OF THE
CAROLINA BACKCOUNTRY

FOLKTALES OF THE CAROLINA BACKCOUNTRY

Ghosts, Beasts, & Lost Treasures

Ray Belcher

PACKS MOUNTAIN
PRESS

Copyright © 2021 Ray Belcher

All rights reserved. No part of this book may be used or reproduced in any manner without the prior written permission of the copyright owner.

ISBN: 978-0-578-31227-9

Cover art and illustrations by Ray Belcher.

Contents

	Acknowledgements	vii
	Introduction	ix
1	The Haunted House That Wasn't	1
2	Ghost Rider of Bush River	5
3	Caesar's Revenge	15
4	Old Nell	25
5	Code of Honor	33
6	The Apple Trees	39
7	The Whistler	47
8	The Oates Place	57
9	The Ones Who Lived	75
10	Return of the Hatchet Man	89
11	The Organist of Liberty	99
12	The Spirit of White Wolf Hollow	109
13	Scratcher	119
14	The Witches	129
15	The Others	141
16	Imported Monsters	159
17	Lost Gold	167
18	Forgotten Treasures	175
	Index	

ACKNOWLEDGEMENTS

While requests for privacy and anonymity have been respected, I am most grateful also to the following individuals for their time, knowledge, and encouragement in the compilation of these stories and legends: Abigale Ogden; Philip Ogden; Jimmy F. Stiles; Dave Pursley; Minnie K. Hollingsworth; Elizabeth Holloway; Lonzo Lovelace, Jr.; Julie Waterson; Croel Suddeth; John Pete Taylor; Robert Black; Martin M. Bryant; Linda Elkin; Carl Belcher; Carrabell Belcher; Pearl Wallace; Broughton Colvin; Henry Clark; Otis T. Holloway; Christopher Jessup; J. D. Belcher; Carra Selent; Grace Selent; Lily Lovelace; Keith Clark; Dr. Roy Jackson; Lorene Fisher; Lonzo Lovelace, Sr.; Jerry Holloway; Charles McGill; Johnny Knox; Johnny Cox; Frank Lee; David Belcher, Sr.; Nem Brannon; David Bunyon Stone; Bruce Dover; S. A. Wall; Jordan Styles; Joada Hiatt; James W. Duncan; Spartan "Sparky" Dickson; and Ansel Hawkins.

Introduction

The South Carolina Backcountry, particularly the rural sections of the upper counties, is a section of the state not as populated with "established" ghosts as the coastal region. Many of the people of this area are and always have been plainspoken and practical, not concerning themselves with inexplicable matters any more than is necessary for resolving the issues and returning to everyday labors. For this reason, many of the seemingly supernatural encounters recounted herein are not well-known and have not been previously published.

This is not a typical "ghost book." The incidents described here involve ordinary people who happened to become caught up in unusual and sometimes extraordinary circumstances. These areas of human experience are hard to pigeonhole other than as lore. To some extent, they represent the borderlands between truth and imagination, neither completely established fact nor yet disproven fiction. For this reason, in this book, no judgment is rendered on the existence of ghosts or monsters nor on the validity of purported treasures herein described. Information is reported as it was received, and human nature must be respected. Most strange incidents occur when we least anticipate them. We are surprised. The odd experience, abrupt encounter, or sudden discovery leaves us momentarily shaken until thought returns and we realize we need to verify what just happened.

If what we earnestly desire is the truth of a matter, we need to apply close observation and critical evaluation of facts from a perspective of open-minded skepticism. Under this kind of scrutiny, many legends and myths may yield to ordinary explanations and lose much of their romance and mystery in the process; but the final revelation may be eminently satisfying when the final truth is learned.

It is a universal need to know and understand that drives humanity to seek answers and explanations, to explore the unknown, and to push the boundaries of knowledge ever farther, even if only incrementally, despite any fears and doubts we harbor. Deep in our being, we feel some primeval sense of reassurance that, no matter what we find, we will be better for it.

Yet, despite its deep and ancient cultural origins and the intense widespread interest it attracts, the paranormal has commanded serious attention of but few scientists. It is extremely difficult to study through the traditional scientific method, which demands repeatable experimentation and a dependable flow of data, neither of which are likely in a field characterized by unique or sporadic phenomena. Instead, the field has been left largely to nonprofessionals who often lack specific training as well as the funding to carry out rigorous study.

Still, over time and often indirectly, some studies in medicine, psychology, and physics have shed light on phenomena once believed to be forever cloaked in shadow or too esoteric to warrant investigation. Most likely, the life sciences will eventually deliver a final word explaining many reported incidents involving ostensibly unknown species, which have managed to remain hidden in an ever-shrinking world. And the disciplines of history, geology, demographics, and geography offer the best methodologies for eventually recovering some of the missing knowledge of human achievement, including locations of "lost" civilizations and legendary treasure troves.

The principal aim of this book is entertainment and, hopefully, some provocation to question, perhaps even a bit of enlightenment. May folktales, where possible, continue to serve as a point of departure for the expansion of knowledge. They rest on not much more than belief but frequently contain germs of truth and occasionally even specific, useful facts that can initiate an ultimate revision of what is accepted as accurate. The epic poetry of Homer, for example, notably the Iliad, held clues leading to the discovery of the location of the once-fabled lost city of Troy and, subsequently, to the reexamination of historical methodology.

Many of the accounts in this book were collected ancillary to historical research, pieced together from regional newspaper articles and public records, and thus have been placed within their historical framework; where possible, the style and perspective of their principal sources have been retained. Because more than one source was consulted in all but one account, they are presented in narrative form. Hopefully, the settings of events will convey to the reader a certain sense of authenticity while leaving their credibility to the reader's best judgment.

FOLKTALES OF THE CAROLINA BACKCOUNTRY

THE HAUNTED HOUSE THAT WASN'T

Scarcely a town in the nation does not have at least one dilapidated, abandoned house commonly regarded to be haunted. In Greenville, between the two World Wars, it was two miles from town on Buncombe Road. The old house had been vacant for years. At least, no people occupied it. Once, it had been a grand place where children laughed in its halls and played under the oaks in its spacious backyard, where a father came home to warmth and meals and love. It had once been a symbol of returning prosperity, built after the Civil War with profits earned from the operation of a New South general store. It was a happy domicile if ever there was one.

But no more. For almost two decades, it had moldered after tragedy had taken place within its walls. The murder had never been adequately explained. The police could not even determine exactly how it had happened. No weapon was ever found, nor was any suggested motive at all convincing. The meager evidence was never sufficient to support an indictment, and the one suspected of being able to shed light on the incident remained mute until death.

Afterwards, the house sat vacant except for the occasional tenant who was offered the house on extremely fair terms. The one room, the murder room, would not, of course, be used. It would be kept sealed. The owner would have the key if it became necessary to open it, but that would surely never happen. Better not to use the room with the indelible blood spot on its floor, out of respect for the dead. Besides, the room was the last on the upstairs hall and very small at that; there were nine other rooms without a stain, plus indoor water and sanitary facilities.

Despite these amenities, few tenants could be found, owing to the house's infamy. Some moved out almost as quickly as they had moved in, citing bumping and shuffling noises in the still of the night, strange vapors and smells, and even sounds of something dripping. The room remained sealed against entrance for all – all, that is, except the spirit, which was said to nightly pass through earth and walls to visit the place where its life had been extinguished.

Every child who walked the road took care to cross over to the opposite side before passing the old house. Even the adults who passed by made sure to do so before darkness enveloped the street in the evening. Neighbors had seen, even when the house was vacant, the dimmest blue light radiating from an upper window late in the night. The light appeared and faded unpredictably; but observers knew, without ever having been in the once-grand house, that the window belonged to the room stained with blood. On occasion, they might see the faint illumination blink, as if something was passing between the light and the window. They were certain they knew "what" caused the strange occurrences in the old house, but not one of them would venture to explain the "why." Who can know why the spirits come and go as they do? The neighborhood was composed of the good and the faithful, who believed that man was not meant to know all things, so they let these kinds of incidents pass. But they still talked about them in guarded fashion, even in daytime when the sun was high.

The house was finally let to brothers, men of the professional class (although no one seemed to know to which profession they belonged). Neighbors speculated that the men could be doctors or lawyers, or perhaps one of each. The house's owner, who did business on the basis of a firm handshake, protected their privacy, collected their money, and only revealed that their name was Smith. The brothers remained in the house much longer than any previous tenants had, obviously unperturbed by any paranormal events that might be occurring within their home. But in the small hours, if a neighbor was stricken with insomnia and happened to cast a glance across the street and up toward the infamous window, the small blue radiance could still be seen.

Passing months turned into years, and the brothers became an almost but not quite normal part of the community. They were rarely encountered on the street. If one or both Smiths happened to be outside when a neighbor passed and issued greeting, they might nod or they might not. The men owned a large touring car, which was parked in the alley behind the house. It was driven at odd hours, but the neighbors remembered that doctors were always on call and let the matter pass from essential thought.

Early one morning in late winter of 1924, the touring car cranked loudly and left. Neither it nor the brothers were ever seen in the neighborhood again. Days later, Deputies King and Cothran drove up in a black A Model Ford and entered the house with the landlord, who was noticeably fidgety. When neighbors saw he was wearing the iron bracelets of the law, they were seized by rising curiosity and followed the trio inside the abandoned house and even up the squeaky steps. The haunted room was finally opened in broad daylight by the turning of a key supposedly unused in years.

As soon as the door creaked open, the deputies confirmed the truth of the matter: the room was indeed filled with spirits. Before them, arrayed in perfect working order, was a complete and recently used gas-powered copper whiskey still, replete with fresh water and an indoor water closet – a flawlessly complete illegal factory.

The mysteries collapsed with the suddenness of death itself. Within two hours, it was known all over town that the house's owner had been in cahoots with the moonshiners; the three of them had encouraged the ghostly rumors to preserve their privacy during the early years of Prohibition. Tenants and neighbors unwittingly cooperated by seeing shadows move about in the "empty" house, smelling wisps of foul vapors, and hearing unaccountable noises. The dim blue light from the low gas flame had been, to some astute scripture readers, proof of a doorway to burning brimstone. Once the story was set straight, neighborhood chatter became much more discreet. Things like illegal stills were not talked about openly or people would think… well, you know what they would think.

When justice was finally served, the city of Greenville lost a little mystery, and neighbors lost a source of delicious conversation; but there remain plenty of other backcountry tales that are not so easily explained away.

GHOST RIDER OF BUSH RIVER

A detailed account of the phantom rider of Bush River dates from 1860, although the oral tradition dates much earlier, to the time of the Revolutionary War. Rather than a terrifying tale, this ghostly romance is an illustration of the power of love. The supernatural element, though important, is incidental to the relationship, which defied the grave's power to end it. The intensity of the times and the passion of the couple demands a grandiose and somewhat sentimental perspective, as it has been passed down.

Bush River is a small tributary to the Saluda, which forms half the water boundaries of the region known as the Dutch Fork. Among the earliest settlers along Bush River in Newberry County were a handful of members of the Quaker faith, who arrived by the 1760s on the Carolina frontier and settled on both banks of the winding river in the vicinity of O'Neill's Mill. One of these settlers was David Miles, a seventy-year-old widower with two children, David, Jr. and Charity.

In 1775, when war broke out in the north between the British and the colonists, political opinions in South Carolina varied greatly. The Backcountry was particularly divided over the question of independence; however, the Quakers of Bush River, including David Miles and his children, were committed to their beliefs and would not take up arms. His neighbors, by then, understood and respected this old man of unimpeachable principles and godliness. David, Jr., was just as staunch as his father; he would remain true to his faith. His musket would be used to shoot rabbits, if anything, not men.

Charity's position was more problematic. A vision of beauty at nineteen, she already had a young man's love, which she willingly returned. Only the war prevented their marriage and settlement into a farmer's life on the banks of the gently flowing river. Her sweetheart, Henry Galbraith, was also a Quaker; otherwise, David Miles could not have allowed him to pay court to Charity, as it would have been "out of union" to do so. Religious views notwithstanding, young Galbraith was moved, perhaps by what he saw as Tory treachery, to support the fight for independence. He vowed he would not kill but would instead serve as a scout and a courier – fitting work for a man who rode well and had a dependable mount.

Couriers were critical to the war effort in the state because the South was becoming increasingly important to the ultimate outcome of the war. Henry successfully carried many missives that contributed to the preparedness and movement of Patriot forces, keeping them safely positioned in strategic locations. His steed, a sleek black stallion, was reputed to be the fastest horse in the county.

Charity and Henry danced on pins and needles during the three years he carried out his duty. Only providence combined with the speed and endurance of his horse saved him from death or disaster many times. The war as it developed in South Carolina was particularly bloody because it divided not only neighbors but, in many instances, families into opposing camps. There was also the problem of changing allegiances; as men lost faith in their leaders, they switched from one side to the other. In this state of affairs, it was hard to tell who one's friends were from one day to the next.

Henry's work became increasingly hazardous with time. Early in the war, when much of the fighting was being waged in the northern colonies, he had been able to spend some time working in his father's fields. Now he was obliged to make himself scarce as demands were placed on his ability and willingness to carry the pouch. South Carolina was rapidly becoming a major theatre of battle, and couriers had to ride, come hell or high water. But despite the hardships of war, Henry and Charity were bound by the kind of undying love that youth and optimism generate.

Henry and his horse had become well-known as prime targets to the Tories, and Henry often made himself absent from the Bush River settlement out of necessity for weeks at a time. Late on a blustery December night after one such absence, as the Miles family sat up – Charity sewing, the old man reading his Bible, and the son cleaning his hunting gear – the sound of hoofbeats could be heard above the wind.

David Miles quickly extinguished the candle, and Charity met the rider at the doorway, taking his hand to bring him into the warm shelter. David, Jr., put more wood in the fireplace, giving enough light for all to see. For several eternal minutes, gazes said more than any words that might have been spoken; only the crackling of the rising fire made a sound.

When at last the silence was broken, David Miles told Henry that he was there at a bad time. The Tories were scouring the countryside for him. With the warning given, David and his son stepped into the other room. Under those conditions, Charity and Henry had but a short time in the late hours to talk. They avowed their love, as sweethearts must each time they meet, and then Charity asked Henry not to return until the war was over. How long could it last? It was not a quarrel, just a plea for him to take care of himself. Henry agreed to stay away – for a time, at least. Not knowing how long the war might last, he promised, "One year from tonight I will be here, living or dead. The grave itself shall not hold me!"

The words frightened Charity, requiring that Henry hold her in his arms and mitigate his words with assurances that he would not take unnecessary risks. Then, with a kiss and a bark of goodbye to David, Henry was out the door and on his horse, melting into the darkness, leaving only the fading clatter of hooves.

Moments later, Charity heard confused shouting in the distance, indistinct but unmistakable. Then, gunfire! Flashes from musket and pistol lit up the distant darkness, and then all was silent except for the whistling wind. Days later, David Miles received word that the Cunningham Tories had nearly captured a Whig courier but that his horse had been too quick for them.

The courier was true to his word and did not return during the allotted time. Meanwhile, the tide of war had turned more than once. The war for independence had turned into civil war in South Carolina. Victory followed loss in as little as two months in great battles at Camden and Kings Mountain. The colonies had, for all practical purposes, won their freedom from Britain, but many Redcoats and Tories did not realize it. There were still skirmishes and acts of terror and revenge in Carolina for months after Cornwallis surrendered, especially in the Backcountry. The Cunninghams continued to raid and kill, savagely attacking soldier and civilian alike.

O'Neill's Mill was not on the beaten path of commerce, so it was mostly news from neighbors who journeyed out and back that had kept the Miles family informed of the progress of the war and now the slowly developing peace. Despite the war having formally ended, there was still no sign of Henry.

December finally came; the anniversary of the sweethearts' parting was as cold and blustery as its predecessor. Wind streamed through the cedars beside the cabin and funneled under its eves, rising in pitch from moan to howl before dying away to repeat the ascent with the next gust.

Charity continued to sit up after her father and brother retired. The hours passed slowly; the candle had burned itself out long before she finally dozed in the rocking chair. The only sounds in the house were made by the occasional crackling of the dying fire in the hearth and David's heavy breathing. Stirring, Charity thought that she should go to bed; but instead, she softly unlatched the door and stood in the cold silence, staring at the silver crescent about to settle among the distant trees darkly silhouetted against the western sky. The wind had diminished to a breeze that rattled the few stubborn remaining leaves on a small maple near the porch. Then Charity heard something else in the darkness. Was it the sound of hoofbeats?

From the faint shadows cast by trees across the field came a dark rider at full gallop in the pale light of the moon. Slowing but never stopping, horse and rider passed not fifty feet from where Charity stood.

"Henry!" she whispered, unable to further articulate the excited thoughts now racing through her head. A second time the name formed upon her lips as the horse and rider whipped past; but not a sound came from the figure on horseback. The coal-black horse, nostrils flared and muscles rippling with each mighty lunge, seemed to fly over the ground, just as it had the last time Charity saw Henry riding away.

Then it was morning, cold, still. Had it been no more than a dream? Did she dare to think he would not keep his promise? Old David scoured the ground and found not a trace of a track to show that any rider had passed by. From a kinder sleep the following night, Charity awoke with the compulsion to again open the door to silent darkness. Alone in the world but completely aware, she stood to hear once more the soft rapid rumble of distant hooves and to watch the dark figure fitfully riding, never pausing before passing back into the blackness. Again he came the following night, and again, and again, just before midnight, whether stormy or fair, his great black horse never faltering.

When horse and rider passed by the first time, Charity knew something was wrong. She remembered Henry's parting words, that not even the grave would keep him from her. Days passed into weeks, then months and years before Charity accepted in her mind what her heart already knew: the rider was the spirit of Henry Galbraith. How and when Henry had died she did not know, might never know, but she knew that somehow he had endeavored to break the bonds of death and fulfill his vow. Nightly she faithfully waited for a brief visit stolen from death. Henry would never return as she had known him, as she had loved him; still, she cherished every moment's enchantment with his spirit.

In time, Charity's experience became generally known. She had not escaped the notice of neighbors. The curious and bold came to try to catch a glimpse of the phantom; and some were apparently not disappointed, for reports of the rider circulated throughout the countryside. He came each night, summer and winter, to ride by the Miles cabin, a spectral reminder of the violence and turmoil that still existed in the Backcountry in the aftermath of war.

Eventually, a peace treaty was signed and measures of justice given to the marauders and murderers who had allowed war to shield their crimes. In December of the year that peace returned to Bush River, on the anniversary of the lovers' parting, Charity sat with her father and brother as the hour approached for her to step outside. They listened as the sound of hooves grew louder, louder than ever. Both men stood with questioning looks upon their faces. Before Charity could reach the door, it burst open, and an illuminated figure, unmistakably the figure of Henry Galbraith, entered the cabin and stood silently. So different he was, covered in rain and sleet. He gazed at Charity with the intensity only love can apply. If he made a sound at all, it was a sigh; then he turned and was in the saddle almost instantly. With a flick of his arms, he was off into the blackness, into the storm.

Charity, peering into the darkness, mesmerized, was startled by her father's touch. "Child?"

She barely heard him, pondering what she had seen and heard, and it was several moments before she finally asked, "You saw him too, Father?"

They sat up the little time remaining until dawn, both men now admitting to a strange encounter but neither certain of what had been seen. They tried to reason, but reason failed. There were as many reasons that it had to have been Henry as reasons it should not have been.

Charity never spoke of the rider again, nor did she ever marry. Her father and brother never made public comment about what they had seen. Old David passed away before the new century turned. Many of the Quaker brethren migrated from Bush River to free territory by 1810, but Charity remained on the small farm by the river. Her brother saw that she was provided for as they grew older.

Neighbors talked about Charity's experience when other gossip was slack. In later years, she was described as odd or peculiar by some who did not know her story; by others, she was known for her kindness and generosity. Despite her eccentricities, she came to be respected by most. Occupied by her duties to God and her earthly chores, Charity lived well into the 1800s. The old cabin aged with her and was never reoccupied after her death, eventually crumbling to dust.

Beyond sight of the Miles cabin, Henry's service was little known. Any glory earned by a courier transferred to some battle commander or frontline hero. As the years passed, no former comrade in arms came by to tell of Henry's fate. No annals of the war recorded his role in the fight for independence. No general nor other officers mentioned Henry in their memoirs or diaries. But Charity knew, and she remembered.

In 1838, eight years after Charity's death, a scholar by the name of Lyman C. Draper began to collect the memories of as many surviving veterans of the Revolution as he could. His vast notes contain accounts of exploits of many couriers like Henry, some likewise killed for the sake of their country. Although Henry's sacrifice has remained anonymous in recorded history, his bravery was mirrored in the actions of his comrades on horseback.

Sightings of the phantom rider continued for decades. Talk abated somewhat after Charity's death, but it was said and repeated for many years afterwards that, on the anniversary of the day of their parting in December, the thundering of hooves could still be heard; and on clear nights, if the moon was right, a dark rider on a ghostly steed could be seen almost flying over the old fields that lie beside the banks of Bush River.

"Caesar"

CAESAR'S REVENGE

Most ghosts are described as anthropomorphic entities which are assumed to have had human form in life; there have also been reported, however, many instances of nonhuman spirits interacting closely with the living. In the Backcountry, one account of a supernatural creature not only illustrates the powerful bonds possible between man and beast but suggests very human motives for these animal spirits, such as loyalty, duty, and revenge.

Clarence Bedell came back from World War II and farmed for ten years before he gave up trying to make a living from the hardest work in the world. He rented a little house that had once been a tenant house and went to work at a mill in Gaffney. When he pulled forty-eight hours in a good week, he could bring home nearly forty dollars after deductions. It was the most he had ever made in a week. It was almost enough to live on.

The house he rented came with five good gardening acres, surrounded by three hundred more in the Soil Bank, much of which had been cottoned to death and lay worn out and contoured by rain-made gullies. Clarence, his expectant wife Ellie, and their two daughters Lynda and Angelea put in a big garden their first year. Each spring afternoon when the weather was good, from March on, the four of them spent their spare hours fighting weeds and bugs and working guano into two acres of tomatoes, squash, green beans, and potatoes. Peddling surplus from the garden and forty or so dozen eggs from the chicken house every week, Clarence believed he stood a chance to get ahead someday.

By late May, it was after eight o'clock before the daylight finally grew too dim to work outside. That was when they saw it the first time. Out of the corner of her eye, Lynda caught a movement at the edge of the trees along the nearer end of the upper field. Angelea followed her sister's gaze and saw a black shape moving out of the distant trees. The only way they could discern it was that it was moving and the trees were not. As it drew nearer, the shape turned into a horse, running at full gallop. It raced along the edge of the row of half-grown corn, moving gradually away from the trees, and then abruptly stopped as if halted by some obstacle. It then reared up, spun around, and galloped back the way it came. After running a hundred yards or so in the opposite direction, it again stopped, reversed course, and resumed in full gallop.

It did this three times as the girls watched in awe. What was wrong with it? The only horses they had ever observed were the big, lumbering animals that drew wagons and pulled plows. Was this one frightened? Was something after it? Again, it raced parallel with the corn rows. This time, however, it did not stop. If anything, it sped up and launched itself upward, sailing into the air as if jumping an invisible barrier before coming down at full speed only to disappear into the darkness of the trees at the far end of the field. The whole scenario had played out in not much more than a couple of minutes.

The girls ran to the barn and told their father what they had just witnessed. Clarence calmed them down. He knew children often get excited and sometimes see things differently than adults. Nevertheless, he believed they had seen something, and it was probably a horse. Animals were bad about getting loose, jumping fences, and winding up where they had no business being, usually at the most inconvenient times.

At supper, the girls wanted to continue the discussion; but it was after nine o'clock, and the morning would bring another day of school. Clarence was sure somebody would come by first thing in the morning looking for the horse; and if the bus hadn't come, the girls could show him the tracks and help him recover his property. Only later, as they talked themselves to sleep, did the girls realize the madly galloping beast had made no sound and raised no dust.

At recess, Lynda mentioned the horse to some of her classmates. They were all mildly impressed but soon forgot about it – all except for a small, dark-eyed girl named Beth. After school, she delayed her walk home and met with Lynda and Angelea in the bus line to discuss what they had seen.

"It was the squire's horse," she told them.

A year and a half earlier, Beth had been riding with her grandpa in his big farm wagon, returning from the town where he had sold two bales of cotton. It had been almost dark when a horse had raced by them in the opposite direction in the field beside the road. Beth had stood up and turned to watch it run. It had jumped a gully with ease before veering off across a newly mown hayfield and disappearing into the shadows. The field was, of course, the same one now planted and tended by the Bedells. Beth had been excited by the speed and power of the animal; but her grandpa, who had seen almost everything in his sixty-seven years, had just casually observed that it was probably the old squire's demon horse.

Beth recalled being scared, but not too scared to listen intently, tucking away the details of the story and asking for more. Beth's grandpa had spent the rest of the trip regaling her with the story he had heard when he was a boy listening to the old men at the country store as they sat swapping knives, telling tales, and chewing their favorite tobacco in the warmth of the massive potbellied stove. As Beth recounted the story, Lynda was convinced that Beth's specter was exactly what she and Angelea had seen.

It was during slave times. Nobody knew exactly when, but a man from Charleston inherited or bought land near the state line about five miles southeast of the Indian path to the mountains. He had a funny name that sounded French; somebody said it ended in a bunch of vowels. His first name may have been Jacques or John, but it didn't matter, because usually folks just called him Jack.

He moved in with his wife and a dozen or more slaves. He seemed to know what he was doing, because he prospered. Most of his neighbors had large holdings, but not as large as his. He had little to do with the other people of the area. If someone had to describe him, the words "arrogant" and "aloof" might have been useful. He wasted no time with socializing and cut his time in church to the bare minimum; after his wife died, he eliminated church from his social calendar altogether.

Not long after his wife's passing, Jack consoled himself with a fine, muscular chestnut stallion with four white stockings. The stallion was a deep-chested animal, built for running and flaunting but certainly not for farm work. Jack named the horse Caesar.

When he went to town, Jack rode his big horse and dressed in his best clothes; he spoke little, and then just to the few people he considered his near equals. It was common practice during antebellum times for a man of high education or in some kind of public service to be accorded the title of "esquire." Despite holding no public office nor prestigious degree, Jack carried himself as though he were king of the county, and people began to call him "squire" mockingly behind his back because of his ostentation.

To set himself apart even further, Jack named his plantation "The Pines" and had one of his men carve out the letters on a broad plank, which he hung from an iron hook at the entrance off the main road. He always referred to his slaves as "my people," implying a compassion that never existed. Jack was not an easy master, and "his people" learned to be quick and humble, because there was little margin for informality, levity, or forgiveness.

The youngest among the squire's people was Marcel, who was small for his twelve years. Marcel was the youngest son of the squire's oldest slave couple. Marcel did not take to farm work as the rest of his family had. His mentor was the squire's overseer, an older hand named George who took perverse pleasure in teaching the boy to do a little mischief. He instructed Marcel in how to work slow, how to disappear, and how to pilfer small amounts of supplies from the storeroom. George didn't see any harm in these tiny crimes, just as long as the boy didn't get caught. And he didn't, not until he crossed a big line.

The one thing George didn't have to teach Marcel was the fun of messing with the squire's horse. Marcel loved the animal and always found some way to be around when George was feeding Caesar or rubbing him dry or otherwise attending to him. Marcel petted Caesar and gave him apples when he could, the only acts of genuine kindness anyone extended to the animal, since the squire expected the same obedience from his horse that he did from his slaves. When the squire caught Marcel dallying at the stable when he should have been working, he cuffed the boy and ordered him back to his chores. The lesson was not learned. One afternoon, Marcel slipped out into the field where Caesar was grazing and managed to get astride the animal just long enough to get caught.

The squire took Marcel roughly to his daddy and made the old man beat the boy. Afterwards, Marcel spent the night locked up without supper in an empty storeroom. The squire was so infuriated that he warned Marcel, if he ever wanted to be a big bad man again, he would be whipped like one.

Thrilled by the speed and power of Caesar, exhilarated by the rush of wind in his face, Marcel became more determined than ever to ride the magnificent animal again. Perhaps the horse, too, felt something as he willingly took a light rider who used neither quirt nor saddle. Marcel never tried to sneak a daylight ride again; instead, he waited until the plantation was asleep. In the moonlight, he clung to Caesar with his knees, his fingers wrapped in the horse's red mane during their secret rides.

Marcel was always careful to lead the horse to the road, where his tracks would blend with the day's traffic, and he carefully rubbed Caesar dry long before dawn. The rides took place near the road, far from the house and the slave quarters. There the grass was thick, the soil soft, the hoofbeats too muffled to be heard at any distance. How long Marcel got away with these surreptitious adventures, no one knew. George had his suspicions and one night followed and watched as the horse came readily to Marcel and stood as the child climbed on its back; but afterwards, George decided it best to keep quiet. Mr. Jack might blame him. Not another soul knew until the night of a gibbous moon in August.

The field was bathed in silver light. The regular course was well-known by both boy and beast. There was a newly fallen tree in the field, not very thick, but a yard off the ground. Marcel knew the horse could make the jump with ease. He didn't see what tripped Caesar, didn't realize a limb had separated from the tree when it had fallen and lay well ahead in the path of the galloping horse. Marcel heard the unmistakable snapping of bone as Caesar collapsed beneath him. The boy was thrown off into the taller grass, shaken but unhurt; the horse could not stand. The urgent sounds of the animal in pain trying to rise awakened the households of slave and master.

There was nothing to be done but to put the animal out of its misery. After shooting his horse, the red-faced squire ordered Marcel shackled and locked in the storeroom for the rest of the night. At daybreak, it was George who was ordered to give Marcel twenty lashes. Marcel's shirt was pulled down so he could receive his punishment like a man.

Take it like a man he did. Although Marcel did not utter a cry, the assembled hands watched him sling his head with each blow, tears flying from his eyes. When he thought the overseer held back, the squire, unsatisfied, snatched the whip and finished the beating, each lick harder than the one before. The child hung motionless during the final blows. When he finished, the squire threw the whip down in the dust and strode off. Before midday, Marcel died in his mother's arms on the straw tick bed in the single room that had been his home.

Sometime around the first of November that same year, George walked to town one morning and asked for a doctor. The sheriff and some other men from town accompanied the doctor after George described the situation.

They found the squire's body as George had found it, slumped against the tall rail fence that had been part of Caesar's enclosure. Other than being shoeless, he was dressed in his good clothes. His face was fearful, eyes frozen in a wide stare, mouth agape; his arms were drawn up and folded across his chest, like an insect in death. From his footprints, it looked like he had run circles around the pen. His strides were long, and there had been many of them. Clearly, his heart had burst from exhaustion, but why had he been running? And barefooted?

George told the men that Mr. Jack had gone down since back in the summer, since Caesar died. He guessed he missed him. And he must have missed his wife, too. That's all George could figure out. The people of the plantation could hear him in the night, sometimes sobbing loudly, other times talking loudly or even hollering when there was nobody else in the house. But the night before had been a peaceful night, cooled with a slight breeze, a good night for sleeping. No one had heard a thing, not even George, who slept within easy earshot of the barn.

The inquest settled on a verdict of death by natural causes, but few believed it; even the six jurymen couldn't figure out anything else to conclude. A severe wound to the left side of his head was the main insult to the body, but the doctor believed it had happened after the squire dropped dead and fell against a post. Somebody observed it looked like the man had been kicked by a mule. Or was it a horse? When George had found the squire, he had thought he saw fresh hoofprints in the pen, some of which seemed to be on top of those of the barefooted squire. There had not been a horse on the property since Caesar was put down, only mules. George didn't mention this during the inquest because it wasn't his place; and besides, there was no sign of any hoofprints when he had returned with the doctor and the sheriff.

Some of the squire's people, the people who had known him best, decided that Caesar had somehow come back to bring the old squire to account for his sins. They never talked about it to the white preacher who sometimes came by for the briefest service, but they had known of things like this happening to bad people. A few thought Caesar had come back looking for Marcel to go on one of their wild rides in the moonlight, but the first interpretation of events proved to be the most lasting. The descendants of the squire's people told and retold the story of the demon horse until it was well-known throughout the vicinity. There were accounts of folks seeing it well into the Twentieth Century, around the time when Lynda and Angelea were children. Naysayers dismissed the tales, pointing out that it was just as likely any old nag that folks were seeing. But how could anyone say for sure one way or another about a horse that raised no dust?

FOLKTALES OF THE CAROLINA BACKCOUNTRY

OLD NELL

White Horse Road, named for a popular tavern once located on the route, is a branch of the state road connecting Greenville to the Saluda Gap. In the 1800s, it more or less followed an ancient Indian path and had been well-used since at least the 1790s by drovers taking herds and flocks of livestock to the markets of the midlands and on toward the coast. Surrounding lands were fertile and desirable as much for their location near the growing village of Greenville as for their agricultural potential. It was there, in the vicinity of Travelers Rest, that William Thurston established a plantation.

Upcountry plantations were based on cotton and operated on principles similar to those applied in the lower part of the state, although the quality and majesty of upcountry homes never approached the ostentation of those of the Lowcountry. Specific conditions were to blame. The upcountry soil was good but less fertile; the lay of the land was not as flat; and the climate was cooler and often wetter. Consequently, upstate plantations produced less cotton per acre, and the cotton produced was not as fine as that grown further to the south. The fall line that divided the state into upcountry and lowcountry also demarcated the state's division between wealth and mere prosperity.

Despite the limited prospects for an upcountry planter, a determined man could buckle down to the hard labor required and eventually build an estate in which he could take great pride. Such was the goal of William Thurston. Records indicate that in 1820 he had no more than four slaves, which meant that he probably worked alongside his slaves in the fields while building his estate. Unlike his lowcountry counterparts, Thurston developed close personal ties with his slaves.

By 1826, Thurston had built a home on a rise known locally as Thurston's Hill. He had a house servant, a woman of middle age, to assist his wife in the household duties and the care of the children. Nell, who had been part of the plantation for several years, had formerly worked as a field hand but had proved responsible and engendered the trust of the family. The children especially got along well with her and called her, with some affection, "Aunt Nellie."

Complex were the bonds that held the personnel of a plantation together in difficult times as well as in periods of prosperity. Although the protocols of a modest upstate plantation differed greatly from the rigid discipline characteristic of lowcountry plantations, uppermost in the minds of many slave owners was the necessity of maintaining proper distance between the slaves and the masters' families. Discipline was enforced as necessary and by a range of means.

But discipline was not an issue on Thurston's Hill. The Thurston plantation was known for humane treatment of its slaves, some would say to excess. William Thurston believed that trust and respect worked both ways. Misbehavior of any kind or dereliction of assigned duties was a rare occurrence. When it happened, a word or two was usually sufficient to correct it.

Nell, in some small way, displeased Mrs. Thurston one Sunday morning. For whatever act it was, the mistress fussed at her beyond what Nell thought was reasonable. On top of that, when it came time for the family to go to church, Nell was told she would have to stay and take care of the youngest child, who had not slept well the night before.

The Thurstons customarily carried their entire workforce to church on Sundays; it was the Christian thing to do. The Thurstons rode in a carriage, and the slaves packed into a farm wagon. The prospect of a free day and socializing with others of their class was a privilege the servants of Thurston's Hill always looked forward to.

Nell was embarrassed and hurt; to her, it was like being punished twice for the same offense. After being scolded, she was being left behind. Not only was she obligated to care for the three-year-old, but she was expected to have the midday meal completed by herself upon the others' return. A stew was hanging, warm, in the hearth; but biscuits, coffee, and maybe a pie were ordered by Mrs. Thurston, inconsiderate of Nell's feelings.

The scolding was a new experience for Nell. She was deeply resentful immediately after it happened and grew angrier as the morning dragged on. There was so much to do. Nell became distracted and careless as she continued to dwell on her plight. She turned over a bucket of water by a clumsy movement before she had half begun and had to get more water from the spring at the bottom of the hill. No well had been dug for the house because there was ample clean, cold water at the spring. It was not too far, but it was all uphill on the second leg, and Nell would have to walk it with two buckets of water on her shoulders. James, the new boy, was in charge of fetching water; but he and the other men were at church, where she should be.

She had no choice in the matter; if she was to do all that had been laid out for her, she needed the water first. She decided to leave the little girl behind, telling her to play in the yard; it was a pretty day.

At the spring, Nell dipped up one bucket of water; but, as she bent to put in the second one, a large blacksnake fell from a small overhanging limb into the water. Nell hated snakes. Terrified, she dropped her bucket and scrambled back out of the way. When the snake harmlessly swam to the opposite edge of the spring pool, Nell retrieved her bucket with a pole. She cautiously dragged the bucket across the smooth bottom, gathering grains of sand and stirring up sediment she had not intended to scoop up. Nothing was going right. She knelt down, lifted the two pails off the ground, rose, and turned to go.

Tottering a bit under the weight of two full buckets, she regained her balance in time to hear a noise, at which she turned abruptly. There was the little girl, who had not followed Aunt Nellie's orders. The proverbial last straw was the instant when the child managed to get underfoot on the narrow path as they started for the house. Nell stumbled around and sidestepped the child but ended up falling hard, spilling both buckets of water.

Nell's temper got the better of her. In a fit of pure rage, she took hold of the child, shaking her violently until she went limp. Nell tried her best to revive the child, caressing her face, massaging her head, and praying. She stopped when she finally realized nothing would help. Nell had killed her favorite of the Thurston children there in the woods surrounding the spring.

When the family returned from church, Nell was found sitting on the ground beside the child's body, crying. She did not try to get away but owned up to the deed when first questioned. She was remorseful and contrite, according to witnesses. She said that she was afraid and had first hidden the small body in the bushes beside the path, but she had then retrieved it rather than leave the child in the cold, wet leaves. After giving a full account, she made apologies and begged forgiveness from God and the family. She never claimed anything but responsibility.

It was extralegal but customary in those days for the owner to take necessary action when a capital crime was committed by one of his slaves and the evidence irrefutable. Thurston had no room for personal feeling in the matter. The duties of his social position required certain delimited action in order to maintain discipline among his slaves and to fulfill the requirements of society for justice. Nell's trial was perfunctory, a mere formality. Her guilt had already been established by her own words.

The Backcountry was not far removed from its frontier phase, and it was customary at the time to execute a criminal at the site where the crime had been committed, if possible. Nell was taken to the home of Thurston's close neighbors and down a winding path to a large tree, just beyond the spring where she had dipped water. There she was tied, hand and foot, and hanged from a tree limb. She strangled slowly, lurching in the air violently at first and then with just an occasional jerk until she became limp. Her executioners allowed her to hang until they were certain no life remained in the body. She was then buried in the woods back away from the spring on the side of the hill. Her grave was not marked, unless one of the slaves later furtively carved a notch on a nearby tree or put a special rock on the site.

The tragedies of both deaths blighted the lives of the entire Thurston household as long as it occupied Thurston Hill. An atmosphere of inescapable sadness lingered heavily over the plantation. The ties that once bound black and white in a semblance of harmony were forever broken, even though everyone on the land knew a grievous crime had been committed and recognized what the laws of man and heaven required. With little hope of returning the plantation to its former nature, Thurston sold his holdings and moved his family out of the state, eventually relocating to Missouri.

In death, Nell did not sleep peacefully, awaiting the coming resurrection of all souls. Sometime after the removal of the Thurstons, sightings of Nell were reported along the road and in the woods near where she had killed the child and was, in turn, killed.

They saw her at the spring first. Several families used the spring for water; it was on Thurston land but available to anyone, much like a well on the side of a country road. The first people who claimed to see Nell were slaves, getting water for their households, who spread the tale to their masters. Other settlers of the area came forward with their own accounts, and soon the community at large began to talk about seeing Nell's form out in the woods.

Before committing the horrible deed, Nell had been like family to the Thurstons – as much like family as custom and law permitted in those antebellum days. In the opinion of some who heard of Old Nell coming back from the grave, she was evidently trying to find the family that she had betrayed, making what efforts she could to leave the place where she was entombed and return to the comparatively better times she had known before.

Others believed she was too mean even for hell and came back only for revenge.

Whatever the reason, Nell's spirit seemed bound to the land on which the spring was located. All the sightings – and there were many in the years after the events transpired – took place in the vicinity of an island of woodland bounded in part by Keeler Bridge Road and White Horse Road.

Nell's grave also became a site of curiosity. Although the grave had been unmarked after her execution, visitors to the area noticed handmade figures, little dolls, and arrangements of rocks placed uphill from the spring. After several months, some noted how odd it was that her grave had not begun to sink as she went back to dust. Was someone or something preserving the remains?

Some claimed to see her body actually hanging from the tree, eyes and mouth open, gagging for breath. Others saw her on the path leading to Thurston's Hill. Still others saw her out on the road that ran to Greenville. More than once, men in groups visited the place of execution to check the grave and make sure she was still in it. Tales had been told of unholy resurrections; that could not be permitted here. When they were satisfied that she had not moved, they piled rocks on her grave, ostensibly to keep animals from disturbing her; after all, she had been laid in the earth without a coffin. But most people who continued to discuss the appearances of Nell knew better: the rocks were placed to hold her down.

Some believed that area slave-owners had conspired to make up the whole thing in order to discourage misbehavior of their slaves, but such naysayers were in the minority. Despite Nell's sorrow at the point of death, word persisted that her spirit was vengeful: she wanted revenge for her own murder and somehow would kill if she could. This rumor helped reduce traffic through what people had started calling "Nell's Woods." The spring became "Nell's Pond," although there was no actual pond except when it flooded. About the only reasons anyone would go through Nell's Woods needlessly were for a dare or to show off for some superstitious sweetheart being courted. Even the educated upper classes extended some credence to the Nell reports because, as Christians, they knew that Satan could command his demons anywhere he wanted and could fool righteous people with strange visions.

Nell's ghost continued to haunt the woods intermittently for decades. A horseman once reported that, while riding past the area one evening, Old Nell had run out of the bushes, leaped up on his horse behind him, and clung to the frightened, fleeing horse for some distance before finally jumping off. Night hunters of possums and raccoons reported their dogs becoming confused and uncontrollable when they tracked near the spring.

The passage of years have dimmed public memory of Nell's Pond and the spirit who lurks in those woods. Expansion and development have changed the way some of the old roads curve. Much of the island of trees, so prominent in the events of two centuries past, has been cut down or divided into smaller stands. There still remain a few ancient oaks in the vicinity, possibly dating back to Nell's time, scattered over various small parcels of land. It is within reason to think that one could be the tree on which Nell died, bound by ropes and by her guilt. Some of these giants have survived the axe, perhaps because they were too majestic or too inaccessible to be cut; but for whatever reason, they have been left to stand sentinel over the dead in the place once known as Nell's Woods.

CODE OF HONOR

A stone's throw from Highway 76 in Pickens County, there sits an edifice known simply as the Old Stone Church. The church itself is remarkable for its history. It was first erected as a wood frame building by a congregation of Presbyterians from the Pickens District in 1790. They called it Hopewell, after the nearby plantation of General Andrew Pickens, hero of the Revolution. Some years later, the church burned to the ground and was replaced by a more permanent structure made of stone in 1802. The stone edifice was used for services until 1824, when a new building was erected in the town of Pendleton. Since then, the stone building has been used only occasionally, preserved for its historical value, and stands guardian over the vast cemetery spreading out southward.

The burying ground, hallowed by God and the bones of faithful patriots, attests to the old Pendleton District's significance as a center of political and diplomatic activity in the early history of the Upstate. A stone fence demarks the final resting site of notable early leaders including General Pickens, Militia Officer Robert Anderson, and John Miller, the English publisher and founder of the Pendleton Messenger. The churchyard also contains the remains of one Turner Bynum, who, according to legend, does not rest peacefully in his grave.

In the haze of early morning, just as the gray skies recede before the yellow brightness in the east, the apparition of a young man can be seen, continually repeating his actions from a fragment of the last moments of his earthly life. He rises from the mist and stands with arms at his side, awaiting an unheard command to lift a pistol and engage in a duel. When the signal is given, he aims, fires vainly toward an unseen opponent with a silent weapon, and then reels and staggers a step or two before collapsing as the dawn breaks complete.

"Dawn at the Old Stone Church"

In the years between the Revolutionary War and the War Between the States, South Carolina's aristocrats – primarily members of the planter class, along with a sprinkling of professionals and large-scale merchants – defined themselves largely in terms of wealth. This class of men was not above administering discipline to their social inferiors in the form of a caning or whipping as they thought necessary; honor and reputation, however, would be endangered in the event of an unresolved dispute between equals. Gentlemen such as these avoided fisticuffs and common rough-and-tumble fighting but instead settled their differences decisively on the field of honor.

Dueling was not a concept original to antebellum South Carolina; the practice had several forms dating back to the age of chivalry in Europe and governed primarily by tradition and custom. As the practice evolved over the centuries, various attempts were made to establish uniform rules. A detailed set of rules, particularly applicable to the southern aristocracy, were written by John Lyde Wilson, governor of South Carolina between 1822 and 1824. This code was widely accepted as the most proper and civilized way for gentlemen to settle issues that could not be otherwise ironed out.

Every opportunity was first taken between those at odds to mend the breech through their friends or associates. If mutual understanding could not be reached or an apology secured from one or the other, then one could demand "satisfaction," which meant the equivalent of an apology and the restoration of honor to the offended party or proof of the assertions made by the offender. If a disagreement reached that point, it came down to decisions of when and where and sword or pistol. Obtaining satisfaction was tantamount to preserving one's lifelong reputation, a matter serious enough to warrant risk of death for gentlemen of the Old South.

Once the decision to proceed had been agreed to by both parties, it was irreversible, pending an explanation or apology by the one giving offense. Any capitulation after a challenge had been issued and accepted would be an admission of dishonor and cowardice. It simply did not happen. Close associates of both duelists would be present to witness the event and see that the protocols were rigidly observed. Because of the seriousness of the meeting, a doctor was often present, although not always.

On August 17, 1832, Turner Bynum and Benjamin Perry met on an island in the Tugaloo River near Hatton's Ford to fight one of the most famous duels in South Carolina history. The site was selected because it was on the border between South Carolina and Georgia, a sort of no-man's land of indeterminate jurisdiction in case any legal authorities attempted to interfere with the duel. Both men worked as editors for rival Greenville newspapers; Perry headed the Greenville Mountaineer, and Bynum, the Southern Sentinel. At the time of their final meeting, Perry was twenty-seven years old, and Bynum was twenty-eight.

During the weeks leading up to the confrontation, the young men had waged a war of words in their respective newspapers over the issue of a state's supposed right to nullify federal law, the relevant law being the Tariff of 1832. Opponents of the Tariff contended that it was unconstitutional and unenforceable and therefore null and void. Perry's arguments in the Mountaineer argued that nullification could not be supported without tearing the nation apart. To blunt some of the impact Perry was having in the Upstate, Bynum published many letters to the editor from nullification supporters. Their editorial content eventually degenerated into personal attacks, which could not be ignored by a gentleman of honor. Only a duel could settle the matter.

The men and their entourages left Greenville separately the day before the appointed time; their destination was about forty miles west of town. As Turner Bynum was leaving town, he stopped to say goodbye to his sweetheart, Malinda McBee, whose father, Vardry McBee, was ironically one of Perry's staunchest supporters. The couple had met during Bynum's visits to the Upstate when he was in college. Malinda sent him off with a prayer in her heart and a knot in her stomach. She never saw him again.

Just after dawn on Friday, the command was given, and the two men fired. Bynum's bullet harmlessly cut Perry's coat, but Perry's bullet tore through Bynum's abdomen. Perry remained erect and watched as Bynum bent, then crumpled to the ground. Perry passed his compliments to the wounded Bynum, expressed his hope for recovery to his opponent's seconds, and then left the field.

By the day's end, Bynum was dead, having passed away in a nearby farmhouse after medical attention proved futile. His friends transported the body back to the old Hopewell churchyard for burial, a rider having been sent ahead to see to the preparations.

Though the church was not used for regular services, the graveyard was consecrated ground. Church elders refused to let Bynum's body be buried in the cemetery upon hearing of the circumstances under which he had died. Instead, they would allow the body to be interred outside the low wall surrounding the grounds. A grave was begun. The day had started fair, but rain moved in while Bynum's remains were being transported to his burial site. Sloppy conditions threatened to mire the wagon.

Travel was a slow, arduous process; the small cortege arrived long after dark. At midnight, having no choice in the matter, Bynum's friends hastily buried the body of the young editor by lantern light in a muddy grave half-filled with water. Words said over the body were few and hasty.

The nullification crisis ended in March of 1833 with the passage of a compromise tariff. The larger issue that had led to the duel, the question of the validity of nullification, was temporarily settled without bloodshed but remained an undecided issue for nearly three more decades.

Since that time, the cemetery of the Old Stone Church has expanded with the passing of generations, and the grave of the young duelist is now near the center of the burial ground. The silence of the churchyard is often undisturbed save for the rustle of leaves or the song of a bird. The matter of honor which cost Bynum his life has long been settled; however, while his body lay in peaceful repose, Bynum's spirit has been otherwise. The misty figure of Bynum can still be seen to reenact his tragic end each sunrise.

No voices are heard, nor the sound of firing pistols. There is no gasp of a wounded man, nor sound of his collapsing body. Alone, his spirit reenacts the tragic tableau. Do his bones not rest easy because of his undignified and possibly unhallowed interment? Is it an attempt to return to the woman he left behind? Perhaps the passion with which he held to his principles allows him these brief escapes from the confinement of the grave to fight for his honor anew. Who can say? The mists curl and dance in strange ways at the beginning of each new day.

THE APPLE TREES

When the day is spent and the dry weather cumulus clouds of midsummer twilight fade from gleaming gold to pale gray, a mournful sound can sometimes be heard coming from beyond the grounds of the churchyard at Motlow. It is not unlike the distant call of a fox kit, of which there are plenty in this section. Nor is it so different from the sobbing, soft whimper of a boy who can never be found.

The Tucker family lived not far from Motlow Church when cotton was the only way for farmers to make a living, and making that living required the toil and sweat of every family member. This was especially true for sharecroppers, who began each season already deep in debt.

Over the years, Milt Tucker had been blessed with a son, Lon, followed by a household of girls. Milt had always dreamed of the time they would grow crops on their own land; and, after years of working for other men, Milt was able at last to buy a small piece of ground. Just as the case had been on the landlord's ground, every member of the family was expected to work the land the family now actually owned. Growing enough cash crops to live on was tough, no matter what the circumstances.

The children all did their part from an early age, but the boy was bigger and stronger, and much responsibility fell upon him at a time when other aspects of his life were changing. The stress of a boy approaching adolescence added to the tensions already present in the household. In the 1890s, farming was serious business; labor was hard, dirty, and sweaty. Cotton prices were as low as they had ever been, and the ever-present threat of bad weather or pests coming in to ruin a harvest could place a strain on even the happiest of relationships. As it was, Milt and Lon found it more and more difficult to get along.

In the past, when the boy acted up or showed out, Milt corrected him the best way he knew. The family was churched, first of all; God had a clear answer to most questions. When the answer was not so clear, maybe it was because the one seeking it had a mote in his eye. The lessons of Sunday school and the sermons that followed were sufficient to govern the girls' behavior, but not so with Lon. When words and persuasion did not have the desired effect, Milt would take Lon to the barn and there administer the strop. Not that Milt was cruel to the boy; Milt remembered his own father using the strop on him a time or two until he got his thinking right. And besides, there probably wasn't a boy in ten miles who had not been whipped sometime or another, even the preacher's kid.

Still, in some cases, there was only so much of this approach that would work. Milt began to wonder if he was too hard on the boy and slackened his reins a bit. But that just played into the devil's hands. As the boy grew older, his attitude degenerated beyond the confused anger associated with a normal shift into manhood; Lon grew rebellious beyond reason. Part of the problem was a group of older boys who lived near the crossroads.

At the crossroads were two small stores, the church and its new parsonage, a blacksmith shop, and a small steam gin that ran every fall. Boyd Murphy did two or three times the trade Hart did; Murphy's store was twice as big as Hart's, carried more merchandise, and offered the opportunity for a little fun. In addition to the wide selection of candies and bottles of cool sarsaparilla, the store had a pool table to attract men and older boys looking for recreation. Most of the farmers and hands had little time for such foolishness, but there were a few in the community (folks called them no-accounts) who found time to waste or, worse still, a little money to gamble on the roll of the balls. At a nickel a game, Murphy didn't mind. No spirits were sold, but the group of young men and boys that hung out there didn't need alcohol to get into mischief. Sometimes their mischief got out of hand, but that attracted Lon's interest even more. He began to hang around and watch them whenever he could escape the cotton fields. He was big enough to look like he belonged, but it was the proverbial "wrong crowd" for a bright but easily influenced boy like Lon. When they invited him to a game one Saturday, he was hooked like a fish.

About the same time, Lon became interested in girls, one girl particularly. Minnie, a neighbor two years younger than Lon and best friend to Lon's sister Shelby, was someone the boy could trust. She was pretty in a country way, with light brown hair, smoky gray eyes, and an innocent smile that revealed a small gap between her front teeth. Lon saw only beauty when he looked at her, and she allowed him to share all his plans and secrets with her.

Turning fifteen, Lon was still not a man but thought he was. He neglected his regular chores too often and was taken to the barn again and again by his daddy. The last time he went, he wrenched away, used a word of profanity, and told Milt he would take it no more. Milt subdued him with some effort and whipped him. Red-faced and in tears, Lon ran off and didn't come back until the rest of the family had gone to bed for the night.

Nobody said anything about the matter the next day. Lon did the work that was expected of him while gravely considering his situation. He had few choices. He had no good plan, yet. He constantly turned over scenarios in his mind that involved permanent escape from the fields, the barn, and the strop. In the dead of night, with his family asleep, he would sometimes manage to sneak out and meet with his comrades in the moonlight at the crossroads, after Murphy had closed for the day. There they talked big and bragged about what they had done, some small parts of their accounts actually true. Lon ate it up. He followed them in their ways and learned the manly vices of smoking, chewing, drinking, cursing, and acting tough. He came to hate his daddy – or, at least, he thought he did – and to resent his sisters, who didn't have to work much by his reckoning and who taunted and teased him. He especially hated them when they teased him about Minnie.

It went on like this for some weeks. Milt came to believe things were getting better between the boy and himself. For Lon, it was entirely different. Lon's brain had been working overtime. On his last visit to church, he told Minnie to be ready; he would soon be leaving home and wanted to take her with him. Minnie was not quite ready for that, but neither did she refuse his suggestion outright. She knew she would not run off, but it was a nice fantasy to fall asleep thinking about. She vowed to herself that, if he did come for her, she would say "no" when the time came.

But Lon never showed up for Minnie. He did not come to church with the Tuckers for three straight Sundays. That's when people really started talking. Some speculated that he couldn't bear to sit on a hard pew because he had made old Milt mad and Milt had taken him on another trip to the barn. Others thought Milt had given Lon a little room to make up his own mind, although most felt that was unlikely, knowing both Milt and Lon. Best guess was that Lon had simply run off.

When more weeks came and went with no Lon, it got around that Lon's mama had caught him taking money from a matchbox where they kept their cash hidden. When she had confronted him, he had up and left. Maybe that's why the Tuckers had gone to pray as a family at the altar that Sunday several weeks back.

The preacher felt it his duty to break up the gossip parties. People were judging, and that was wrong. Besides, he had seen the boy standing outside the church not a week ago. He was going to speak with him, but when he turned to go that way, the boy was no longer there. He asked around, but nobody owned up to knowing anything about the boy's whereabouts. The preacher, following his own admonition, had to drop the matter.

For a while, the people of Motlow talked about the Tuckers, trying out various theories about their bad son and their strange ways. But eventually, the Lon Tucker story diminished in relevance and faded away amid more widespread talk of plummeting cotton prices, the next election, and war.

Minnie never forgot her first love, although she and Lon had never expressed such sentiments to each other. Lon had never kissed Minnie, nor even held her hand, but she could imagine how wonderful either experience would have felt. She imagined what running off with him might have been like, not realizing that the fantasies sweethearts cherish about each other are often improbable if not impossible. As time passed, she couldn't remember, try as she might, if he had actually ever gotten close enough to touch her.

In the years after Lon's disappearance, as she grew to womanhood and took on the roles of wife, mother, and grandmother, Minnie allowed the occasional thought to drift through her consciousness about the daring plan Lon had revealed to her; and after she became a widow, she thought frequently about the tow-headed boy with the determined half-grin who had proposed to her when they were both children. She often imagined that she heard his voice whisper her name as she walked the path beside the church, especially on warm evenings in late summer. It was pleasant. Was he somewhere still thinking of her after all these years?

It was not until many years later, at the deathbed of her best friend Shelby, that Minnie learned the truth of what had happened to Lon, and her castles in the air came crashing down. Shelby revealed that things in the Tucker household had been worse than anyone outside the family could know. Resentment and jealousy had moved Lon to fight with his sisters, physically hurting them more than once, and to steal a portion of what little money the family had managed to accumulate.

The younger girls were still in bed when Lon slapped his mother in the kitchen that Saturday morning. Milt started toward the boy in a rush. Lon whipped around, yanking out his pocketknife. He barely cut his daddy on the hand before Milt, reacting in a heartbeat, grabbed a stick of stove wood out of the bucket and struck down his son on the spot. He had no time to think, no time to hold back. Shelby had heard her father utter those words many times in his hours of despondency.

THE APPLE TREES

They buried Lon behind the barn in the darkness when everyone else was asleep. The ground was smoothed flat, and the fresh earth was concealed with brush until the rye Milt sprinkled on top had sprouted. Later, Milt planted four apple trees, both to protect the grave and to draw attention away from it. Let the rumors answer any questions that might come up.

Minnie thought that working the field and tending the garden the next season must have been beyond painful for Milt and his wife, knowing what was, to them, in plain view. But they were church people, and Exodus was clear about such matters, even if it brought them no comfort, no relief: "… he that smiteth his father, or his mother, shall be surely put to death."

Lon not only died in his sins but was buried apart from his kin and without proper words – forever beyond the reach of salvation, so many would have believed, had they known the truth. Such folk dismissed the strange sound heard as they headed for the church door as simply the wind whipping through the branches of the apple trees; but Minnie, who heard it many times throughout her life and always thought of the tow-headed boy, knew better.

FOLKTALES OF THE CAROLINA BACKCOUNTRY

THE WHISTLER

In the heat of the early afternoon on Tuesday, August 15, 1899, Ed Hayes hit the road that passed over the Middle Tyger River into Glassy Mountain Township. He had no particular destination in mind but was hoping to line up some work for the days and weeks ahead. Ed was young, single, and willing to work but not yet ready to settle down.

The area where Ed came from around Glassy and Hogback Mountains, called the "Dark Corner," was largely composed of some of the poorest farming land in the state. Ed might have stayed at home and helped his father put in crops, except that he understood it was better that he find employment working for others instead of staying on and being a burden to his large family. He did not mind; this kind of life gave him joy and freedom to roam, pick up news, meet up with his friends from time to time, and meet unattached females.

The young ladies of the Dark Corner found Ed singularly attractive. He was slim with a heaping bush of reddish brown hair that made him look a couple of inches taller than he actually was. Ed was observant, and he was sharp. He was the kind of fellow who had a gift for making almost anyone he met smile, if not laugh. Most appreciated his sense of humor; only a few did not.

Ed was well-known in Glassy and Highland townships as a genial, popular fellow who liked to cut up with kids even though he was in his twenties, way beyond childhood. He was widely known for his habit of whistling as he walked roads from one job to another. Ed was not afraid of work; when he found work, he was assured of a place to sleep and board. His sleeping quarters were usually in barns and haylofts, but during the cold months, he could usually count on being allowed to put down a pallet in the house. Meals were not fancy but filling, and he took them with the families. He would collect a quarter or half dollar for a full day's work, and every day was pleasant because it was different. Hayes followed this path from the day he turned sixteen until a tragic intersection with destiny.

That afternoon, as Ed Hayes strolled down the road, he had the world to himself; the countryside he was in was both secluded and sparsely populated. Just before he began a long descent toward the river bottoms, he stopped to exchange greetings with John McKinney, who had hired Ed for several little jobs over the years. The two made small talk, and Ed told John he planned to go to a revival meeting later that evening.

Ed never made it to the revival, nor was he ever seen again. It wasn't determined that he was missing for several days because of his habitual wandering and sporadic work schedule. After nearly a fortnight, Ed's name was mentioned at the gristmill and may have been brought up at Pittman's or another of the tiny stores on the roads leading out of the mountains. Even when it became generally noted that Ed Hayes was strangely absent from the community, there were no organized protocols to follow for reporting missing persons nor for organizing a search. Of course, some said with a wink, there was a possibility that Ed wanted to be invisible for a while; it was not unheard of at all for a man of Ed's age and popularity to get out of public sight for a day or two at a time, for personal reasons.

Ed's friends became concerned when he didn't show up at some of his usual rendezvous sites to discuss their mutual exploits and complain about work, weather, or women. Some of them set out to look for him, starting where he had last been seen. On August 30, J. M. Farmer and others discovered a badly decomposed body in a shallow grave several hundred yards upstream from the bridge over Middle Tyger River. It was tentatively identified as Ed Hayes because of the clothing: Ed had been last seen wearing overalls and a fairly new blue chambray shirt; and, although the shirt could hardly be called new anymore, the color looked about right. A more certain determination could not be made at that time, however, for the recovered body was headless.

The men went back into the woods, searching for the head, but it was not found in the grave nor anywhere nearby. A day or two later, while inspecting a patch of peas and cane, Luther McKinney discovered a skull that looked as if it had been carelessly thrown into the field like something disgusting.

When the parts were assembled, Dr. J. H. Lindsay performed an autopsy and completed identification of the corpse with assistance from Ed's friends. Overall size, build, teeth, scars, and strands of hair still attached to the skull all indicated that the body belonged to Ed Hayes, and evidence pointed to him having been killed violently. He had been shot at least twice in the torso, once very close to the heart, which had probably killed him. After his death, his head had been neatly severed from his body. Due to the condition of the body, no other wounds nor any other possible cause of death could be ascertained.

An inquest was held, presided over by Judge M. L. Gullick acting as coroner. Witnesses helped piece together Ed Hayes' final days. It was determined that Ed had last been working for James Suddeth in Highland Township, doing general labor. Witnesses surmised that Hayes probably slept in the barn, since the Suddeths had six children and one on the way. He had stayed with the family for several weeks prior to the day John McKinney saw him, and he had expected to work at least until sometime in September.

Four witnesses swore they had heard James Suddeth either threaten to shoot Hayes or admit that he had shot him. Based on abundant testimony, Judge Gullick found that Ed Hayes had been killed with a pistol by James Suddeth and ordered the sheriff to arrest Suddeth.

Trial was held in February of 1901. Initially, some of the witnesses for the prosecution proved reluctant to give testimony in court and had to be subpoenaed and subsequently arrested. Ultimately, there was no shortage of witnesses to Suddeth's threats or to his admission of the crime. It was further established that Suddeth owned a .38 pistol, that Hayes' body was found on land that Suddeth farmed, and that Suddeth had been seen coming armed from the bottomland where the body was found about the time Ed Hayes was killed.

Suddeth's defense was weak, at best. He did not confess to killing Hayes, but he also did not deny it. He simply stated that there was no hard feeling between Hayes and himself. He added, unfortunately for his case, that he had hired Hayes under the condition that Hayes stay away from his wife. Everybody knew how bad Hayes was after the women. Finally, in what to the jury must have seemed an act of desperation, Suddeth's wife testified that she had seen Hayes walking the road, unwounded, after the date of her husband's alleged actions. She was uncertain as to when that sighting was, but it was after Hayes was supposed to be dead. No one corroborated her account.

The prosecution constructed a scenario of Suddeth, jealous of the perceived attention Hayes was paying to his wife, ambushing or encountering Hayes that afternoon and firing until Hayes dropped. Then, fearful of being caught, Suddeth tried to hide his crime by concealing the body and obscuring its identification by removing the head. Suddeth maintained silence in the courtroom as this scenario was presented. The prosecution did not attempt to prove any illicit relationship, for Suddeth had already done enough damage by supplying a motive.

The jury found the evidence overwhelming. The most difficult matter for decision was Suddeth's state when he committed the act. If it was an ambush, then it was planned and clearly first-degree murder. If he had acted in a fit of passion, it was manslaughter. The jury came to the conclusion that, while some premeditation was evident, Suddeth's actions also appeared sudden and rash, coming after having employed Hayes for weeks. Suddeth was found guilty of murder with a recommendation for mercy and received a sentence of life in prison. It was while he was in state prison that the rest of the story came out; Suddeth befriended another long-term resident who eventually shared the tale.

Suddeth had the impression that there had been talk in the community about Hayes and Suddeth's wife. The more he thought about it, the madder he became, not just because of his wife's supposed infidelity, but because people thought he had been cuckolded. He planned to catch Hayes away from the house and give him a good whipping. Ed Hayes picked up on the danger and left without notice the day of his death. Suddeth followed him, staying off the road in the brush, until they reached a stretch in the road Suddeth judged would be far enough away from prying eyes to confront Hayes. He jumped out of the bushes and ordered Hayes to stop. When Hayes didn't, Suddeth fired at him, hitting him at least twice.

On the spur of the moment, Suddeth, believing rightly that he would be implicated if Hayes' death were known, cut off the head of his victim with a knife and threw it into a cane patch across the road. He then picked up the corpse, slung it over his shoulder, and headed for the river, not far away. He had rented a piece of bottomland from Perry Barton and planned to put in a turnip patch there on the north bank of the river.

With his burden slung over his shoulder, Suddeth slogged through the underbrush beside the river. The sky darkened, distant thunder rumbled, and the wind picked up with the threat of a storm. As the gusts blew harder, Suddeth heard a new sound – a hoarse whistle that came and went with the wind. Suddeth continued to walk, faster as the storm approached. The strange sound came on stronger and sounded nearer. It was coming from the body on his shoulder! The dead man was trying to whistle! Suddeth threw down the corpse and backed off, terrified of the coarse sound that came from the body.

He stared at the corpse in horror and listened. Somehow the wind, blowing over the gaping throat of the murdered man, was producing a sound not unlike a whistle. Even piled in a heap on the ground where Suddeth had dropped it, the body continued to whistle with each fresh gust. The sound was not a melody by any means, like the one Ed Hayes had whistled just before Suddeth confronted him, but it changed pitches as the wind played over the dead vocal cords, producing what sounded like a signal to alert someone of the murder.

Suddeth, now severely spooked, searched in a panic for a spot to get rid of the body. He almost couldn't stand to touch it again. The dirt of the riverbank was soft. He fell on his knees and began clawing the earth with his hands until he had a decent-sized hole; then he dragged the body over and shoved it in, touching it as little as possible. He hurriedly raked sand and leaves over the makeshift grave, stomped it down, and left, never noticing if anybody else was around.

He reasoned that it would soon rot in the heat and humidity of summer. Any flooding of the river would further the destruction of the body and maybe even carry it away. If it were found, it could not be identified, since Suddeth had been careful not to leave anything in a pocket – no papers, change, or knife. The deed done, he went home for supper and spent the first of ultimately thousands of sleepless nights beset by visions of the man he had killed.

Ed Hayes proved to be just as restless in death as he had been in life. Maybe Mrs. Suddeth had actually seen Ed Hayes after her husband killed him. He was later reported to have been seen at half a dozen sites between Campobello and the Hendersonville Road in the months following the murder. People who were used to seeing him in life continued to see him in death on the roads that he had frequented. One report had Ed out in a pasture near Berry's pond. Theories about Ed's presence circulated with some regularity around the Dark Corner. Some believed his spirit was looking for his head and didn't yet realize that he was dead. Others thought he was going to the Green's farm or the Howard place, where he had found work in years past.

Every once in a while, someone who saw Ed was so convinced of what he had seen that questions popped up. Was Ed Hayes really dead? Could the body have been someone else? The magistrate and local doctor were questioned about the possibility of mistaken identity. Both maintained they were satisfied the body was that of Hayes. Many others had verified the fact by its physical features and the salient fact that Ed had never shown up for work anywhere after that mid-August day.

Some folks explained that it was Old Chadwick Howard who had been seen, not Ed Hayes' spirit. Called the Hermit of Dark Corner, Chadwick Howard had taken to loafing the hills and highways near his home on Glassy Mountain since becoming a widower. He had no immediate family, having lost his wife to illness and his sons to crime. Said to be "childish," he was sometimes found bundled up in the brush and leaves for his night's lodging. How he managed to get along was a wonder, but it was known he took charity from his neighbors and distant cousins. Yes, he could easily have been mistaken, especially from a distance, for Ed Hayes.

The only problem with this explanation is that Chadwick Howard died in 1912, and Hayes sightings continued to be reported into the 1930s. Hayes was usually seen off the side of the road, seeming to be paying close attention to some feature of the land, such as a broken fencepost or a leaning tree. He would always be turned away or stooping over; and even when a car passed and the driver blew his horn, Ed usually didn't turn or respond in any way. But if the window was down and the driver's ears alert, a whistle might be heard: not a tuneful whistle; just a coarse, shrill note or two like that of an eight-year-old boy trying to get the airflow right without having the necessary teeth.

And if there were still any doubt in the mind of the passerby as to whether he was seeing the spirit of Ed Hayes, all doubt would be removed as the roadside stranger stood erect and slowly turned toward the approaching vehicle; for only Ed Hayes could whistle without a head.

FOLKTALES OF THE CAROLINA BACKCOUNTRY

THE OATES PLACE

The story of the Oates place is recounted here as it was told to me, by the woman who had lived there. Many years had passed between the strange events that marked her childhood and the time of her telling; but the memory and mystery of what had happened had not been dulled.

The Oates house was one of the finest places we had ever lived. We arrived there in February of 1914. I was seven that year. There were eleven of us altogether, ten Dovers and a Stuart. Besides Daddy and Mama and Grandma Stuart (Mama's mother), there were eight children in the house: William, Irvin, Robbie, Marcel, Lily, Alice, Ollie, and me. I am Julie Ann.

Daddy was a sharecropper, and we were a poor family. We owned no land nor a home. Daddy farmed another man's land in exchange for being allowed to live in the house and keep half of all the crops he raised. The last few years had been hard ones for us. Some years there was too much rain; other years, there was not enough to make good crops. We had stayed on one place since I was five, and Daddy had a couple of good years; but the land got poor because we couldn't get enough guano, and Daddy wanted to try somewhere else. He heard about the Oates place and checked into it.

A Mr. Oates had built the house and owned the land many years ago, but Mr. Belt Anderson was the present owner. It turned out nobody had farmed the place recently; the land, all thirty-something acres, had lain fallow now for well over a year, maybe more. Letting the land lay for a spell enriches it. That's what Daddy said. So he got in touch with the owner, and we started packing. It didn't take much packing, because we didn't have all that much.

We were thrilled to have found such a nice farm to work. I could see with Daddy's eyes how nice and flat much of the place was. There was a road that curved a little toward some woods and then out of sight over a small hill. A thin line of trees seemed to march up the hill almost to the back of the house. Two big fields stretched out to the left and across the road to the trees on another little hill. The nearest house was just visible on the horizon, standing maybe a third of a mile away; and the steeple, just the steeple, of the church could be seen far up the road if you squinted and knew where to look.

The house was much better than the tiny cabins and clapboard shacks we were used to. It had two stories, lots of windows, and a spacious back porch overlooking the fields to the south that led downhill to a creek. Upstairs were two big rooms and a wide hallway between them, almost as big as another room. A wide stairway led up to the hallway; it was the first thing you saw when you opened the front door. It was very fancy, with banisters on both sides of the stairs curving out in opposite directions at the bottom.

THE OATES PLACE

It was the biggest house we had ever lived in. Mama said she'd never known of anybody renting out such a big house. It was the kind of house the landlords lived in instead of the tenants. It was big enough so we girls could have a room to ourselves, as could the boys.

There was an enormous kitchen out back, where Mama and Grandma could bake biscuits and pies and maybe fry a chicken some Sundays. The kitchen was made up of one big room and a pantry. The floor was almost slick-smooth, a sure sign that many a broom of fine sand had cleaned it, year in and year out. There was a rack that at one time could have had twenty pots and pans hanging from it; Mama could only fill up a quarter of its space. The fireplace was as wide as Daddy was tall; I bet you could have cooked a whole hog in it if you had one to cook and could rig up a spit. The windows were intact and could be raised or lowered. That would be a blessing when summer came.

Besides the house, there was also a good barn, a chicken pen, and a shed with a good bit of well-seasoned firewood under it that we could have for no charge. Daddy was proud that he got such good terms on the place and figured it was because he had brought plenty of hands to help with all the field work. He would get two-thirds of the crop instead of the usual half.

Daddy, a lean and lanky countryman with a bushy mustache, had big hands and was as strong as an ox. He and the boys moved our plunder – that is, our household belongings – into the house from the wagon we had borrowed from Uncle Bob Alexander, our own wagon not being big enough to get all of us and all of our things in it at one time.

I said we didn't have a lot, but we brought along quite a bit for a poor family: bundles of clothing and shoes, bedding, a crate of chickens, two pigs, a wash stand, a small chest, two lamps, a lantern, a small crate of dishes, a wash pot, two frying pans, a soup pot, a kettle, several wooden spoons, a churn with a broken dasher, a cutting board that had been just about cut up, a washtub, a feed bucket, and a treadle sewing machine that Daddy had bought off a man in Union and fixed up for Mama. All that, along with part of a barrel of flour and a few cuts of pork and fatback wrapped in cheesecloth, pretty well rounded out our load. Daddy carried a few of his own things in addition, such as his gun and powder horn and a few hand tools.

"The Oates Place," courtesy of Robert Black

We immediately began to explore the place, and the ones who weren't big enough to help with unloading played for hours in the yard because, even though it was still winter, it was a mild and sunny day when we moved in. The next day, Daddy planned to plow if it was dry enough, and we children would go to school whether we wanted to or not. Mama would walk to school with us and then go by the store to look (just look!) at a piece of cloth; the boys' clothes were looking a little ragged. Grandma would set the house in order and get it ready for our family's new life.

Grandma told us she missed us when we got back home that next day. It had been cloudy; and with all of us gone or working in the fields, Grandma would have found the place downright bleak if it hadn't been for the work. She told us in detail what she had accomplished; she liked to do that so we would understand she was pulling her weight. Grandma was short and a little beyond plump but quick on her feet.

Grandma said it more than once over the course of the next several days that she guessed she'd just have to get used to the place; it just seemed odd to her at times. Maybe it was the size; she had never lived in such a large house before. It was so big it had echoes that sounded almost like somebody talking. Grandma reported at the table little things that she noticed as she got to know the place better; it was not quite as fine as it had appeared in the sunshine on the Saturday we had moved in.

Structurally, the house was sound, give or take some loose shingles on the roof and a broken hinge on the back door. A couple of the window sashes were crooked, some glass was cracked, and the porch had a weak plank or two that we had to avoid if we didn't want to be walking on the ground trying to get in the door. There was also a faded stain on the floor of the parlor that Grandma couldn't scrub off, no matter how hard she tried.

Grandma took care of the family's money since Daddy lost a case quarter somewhere between the store and the last house we lived in. He'd straightened up with Mr. Moore, the storekeeper, and gotten twenty-eight cents after trading a really fine fox pelt and some early bell peppers for some salt and sugar. He slipped the money into his pants pocket, but the pocket unfortunately had a tiny hole in it. It doesn't take much of a hole to lose a quarter, but what made Daddy mad was that the pennies had stayed in the other corner of his pocket. Why couldn't they have fallen somewhere in the dust and the quarter have stayed in? He sent two of the boys to look for the quarter, but they never found it. Those two bits would have made a difference, too. Still, we had been lucky; over the last four years, we had been able to save up a tremendous amount of cash money. Counting the five silver dollars and four tightly rolled-up bills, we had accumulated almost fourteen dollars. It was the most money we had ever had at one time.

Grandma usually kept our money in a Bull Durham bag in the bottom of her knitting bag, but she later decided to hide the money in the bottom of the ragbag, a bag of scrap cloth that we used for everything from washing ourselves to bandaging cuts and scrapes. The ragbag hung on a nail on the back porch beside several other items, such as the drinking gourd, a piece of clothesline, a claw hammer, and Daddy's hat. Grandma reasoned that nobody who came along to steal would think to look outside the house, especially not in a ragbag. And why would anyone come to steal from us in the first place, as poor as we were?

It seemed to turn chilly all of a sudden one evening. The fire was burning low in the parlor fireplace, but Daddy brought in an armload of wood just in case. The distant clouds threatened bad weather long before sundown. Sure enough, the wind picked up from the north and howled against the eaves. Hard pellets of sleet began to beat against the roof and sides of the house. Daddy opened the door to take a look, and I could see a few flakes of snow mixed in. We laid down early that night because bed was the warmest place to be. By nine o'clock, everybody in the house was snuggled under covers.

Over in the night, we were awakened by a loud crash. Daddy got up and looked to see if a door had blown open but found the house locked up tightly. Maybe it had been winter thunder, which happened from time to time. It was not of great concern, and everybody rolled over and went back to bed – except Grandma. At breakfast the next morning, she said that she had heard someone moaning all night and that it had kept her awake. She had gotten up to check on the boys, but it wasn't one of them, so she thought it must have been Daddy.

"It wasn't me, and we didn't hear any moaning," said Daddy. "It was probably just the wind. It really howled there for a long time."

"I know the difference between the wind and someone moaning with a bellyache," said Grandma, "and if nobody is going to tell me anything, I will just hush about it."

Two days later, Daddy hitched up Dob to the turn plow when the sun was just beginning to cut through the mist and walked down the backside of the property where the bottom three or four acres sloped down to the woods. The field was in rough shape. It had not been tended in a long time, and there were some little pines in the edge of the field that Daddy had not seen when he first dealt with the owner. Most of the ground was still too soggy to plow, but Daddy and Dob turned over two full two acres before they hit the wet streak and Daddy decided not to plow any more that day. Anyhow, it was closer to supper than to dinner, and he was ready to return to the house for a plate of whatever the womenfolk had fixed.

When Daddy got the mule unhitched and everything put away and finally arrived at the back porch, Grandma met him at the door and scolded him for playing tricks on them. Why had he come around knocking on the door and walls of the house like a stranger and then run off? It was a child's game. She'd have blamed me or one of the boys, except we had all been in the house together when the knocking began.

Daddy looked at Grandma and then at Mama, who joined her, and told them that he had not played any tricks.

"I was unhitching the mule in the barn," he protested. "I am too tired to play tricks on anyone."

Daddy loved Grandma and loved to tease her sometimes when he was in a jovial mood. Grandma sometimes told Mama that she had married a little boy in a man's body, and they would laugh about it. But I watched Daddy as he told them he had not done any knocking, and I believed him; he was beat from his day's work. Mama finally said the knocking must have been the wind or a loose shutter. What else could it have been?

That night was the second time we heard a big crash, like an explosion. It came from the kitchen in the middle of the night and awoke everybody. It sounded like a bunch of pots and pans had hit the floor, but that couldn't be, because we did not have a bunch of anything. When Daddy and Mama looked in, the kitchen was in perfect order; everything was in its place on a hook, nail, or shelf.

In the days following, Mama and Daddy and Grandma reported at breakfast hearing too much running around in the night. Grandma warned us kids to empty our bladders before we laid down; there wasn't any use of us stomping around after the slop jar like that. I don't know about the rest of them, but I was so wore out, I slept through just about every night. I didn't get up and didn't hear anything.

The weeks passed by fast. The ground dried enough for Daddy to get the cotton and corn in; then he planted potatoes with everybody helping. As the days got longer, the corn and cotton started to look promising. Late in May, the rains made the weeds grow in the vegetable garden, and since Mama and the girls were in charge of that project, Mama spent a lot of time out there. One day while she was hoeing the ragweed, dock, vetch, and wiregrass, she heard a jingling noise. The money in the ragbag was clinking. Someone was after the family savings! Daddy was way out in the field, and Grandma had walked to the store for a spool of thread, so it was up to Mama to confront the thief that was stealing our money.

She ran to the house, armed with a hoe, and, before turning the corner, swung the tool back into position to clout the thief on the porch. Heaving for breath, she jumped out from around the corner with the hoe held over her head and saw – not a thing. Not even a breeze was stirring. She looked up and down the road in both directions, but there was no one in sight. She looked around, careful not to draw attention to the sack until she was certain she was alone. The ragbag was not moving and was tied shut, just as Grandma had left it months before. Mama took out some rags and felt around in the bottom of the bag until she felt the coins, still wrapped up. There was no mistaking what Mama had heard; money was so scarce that the sound of rattling coins was distinctive. When she told Daddy and the rest of us about it that night at the supper table, he said that she might have scared the thief off and that he would be more watchful. But Mama was bothered because she had seen absolutely no one.

Several more weeks passed without anything more exciting happening than an infestation of cutworms and beetles in the vegetables. Despite that, we got in the best crops we had ever raised. Daddy promised to take some of the extra produce to the store and swap it for a little candy for us kids when he got around to it. School was out for the session, and we had to do our part in the fields. One day, Ollie got to feeling bad and became irritable. Mandy was told to keep her in the house during the afternoon while Daddy and the rest of us finished the field work. Since we children could handle the little remaining work, Grandma and Mama were free to walk down to visit the minister's wife.

Around midafternoon, Ollie finally settled down for a nap, and Mandy dozed off. She awoke to a moaning sound coming from the loft. It was not a human sound but more like that of a horn. Daddy owned a horn, an old cow horn that had been carved to make a sound like a trumpet; Grandpa had used it to call the dogs back when he went coon hunting. Ollie woke from her nap and began to whimper, but Mandy had heard a hunter's horn before and was not immediately disturbed. One of the boys must have got it and was playing with it. Our brothers were like their daddy in that they let their fun run loose sometimes.

Mandy told us later that she fussed at the source of the sound, threatened Daddy's belt, and then finally pleaded with it to shut up. When it kept on, she gave vent to her Stuart temper and started hitting the walls to irritate whoever was blowing on the cow horn in the attic. Needless to say, none of this commotion did Ollie any good. She got more and more discombobulated and began to cry in earnest; so you had a moan, some wall beating, and a crying child who started laughing when her sister ran around beating on the walls, all sounding off at the same time.

The sound ceased before we got in from the field. Mandy fussed at the boys for waking Ollie, but they had no idea what she was talking about. In fact, it couldn't have been any of them doing it. I know because all three boys were sweating like pigs out in the field with Alice, Lily, Daddy, and me, pulling weeds, picking off bugs, and heaving rocks out of the furrows. But before we broke out into a general argument, Grandma and Mama came in with some fresh-baked cake the pastor's wife had sent over, and the matter of the horn was dropped like a brick. An hour later, full as ticks and worn out from the day's work, we bedded down for the night.

In the middle of the night, the horn started up again. Everybody knew then that Mandy had not imagined the sound earlier. We heard our parents scrambling around downstairs. Daddy and Mama checked the doors first thing, then the windows to see if a dog was baying at the moon. Daddy opened a door to see how bad the wind was, but there was no wind. The sound was coming from the upper part of the house, in the loft. Daddy appeared at the top of the stairs in his long-johns, holding a lantern. He climbed up the loft ladder, which was nailed to the wall, and started raising the loose planks covering the hole. When he raised up the first board, the sound moved away to the other end of the house. Daddy looked at Mama and said, "Somebody's up there with my horn."

Daddy couldn't raise the lantern, hold up the board, and hold on to the ladder at the same time, so he climbed up another rung, about halfway into the loft, and called down to Willie, the oldest, to bring him his shotgun. Willie ran back, got it, and handed it up to Daddy, and then Daddy disappeared into the darkness. He could not stand up in the loft, for the pitch of the house was such that he could easily bang his head in the dark. We could see the light flashing crazily as he tried to crawl while carrying the gun and the lantern.

The dim rays of the lantern did not go far and were swallowed up by blackness in all directions. If Daddy looked at the flame, he was momentarily blinded. He continued to hear the sound and, now armed, crawled toward it. Daddy wasn't afraid of anything. He instructed Willie to thump the ceiling where the sound was coming from and flush it out where he could draw a bead on whoever was making the noise. For a good ten minutes, Daddy played a game of hide-and-seek with the unknown source of the moan; Daddy crept around with his lantern and shotgun while Willie thumped on the ceiling with a stick underneath, and the sound, changing pitch ever so slightly, moved about from one part of the loft to another.

And then it stopped.

We heard nothing else, no creaking boards or footsteps. Daddy held out the lantern in the general direction the last noise had come from and stared into the dim light, trying to focus on somebody crouched or lying down in the darkness, but had no luck. When he came down from the attic, he found every member of the family gathered at the foot of the ladder, waiting for news. Mama and Grandma were clutching us children, as many as they could clutch. Willie was still firmly holding his stick of wood. All of us had big, expectant eyes.

Daddy looked at Willie, saw he had a loop of leather over his shoulder, and asked him, "What have you got there, son?"

Willie brought the loop off his shoulder and held up an object that sent a chill down my back: it was Daddy's horn. Willie said it was there with the shotgun when he had gone after it. Daddy swallowed hard and tried to calm the family. I don't know about the rest of them, but I was not calmed. Daddy tried to explain that it must have been the wind shifting and blowing under loose shingles, but everyone knew it was a still, windless night. We all returned to bed, but few slept the remaining hours until dawn.

The days passed slowly after that night; it took a long time for the events of the summer to move out of our minds. Work helped, though. When cotton time was upon us, we fell into our beds each night. Even a tornado riding a freight train could not have awakened me after dragging a cotton sack for ten or twelve hours in the hot sun. It had been a good crop year. The knocking on the door, the rattling of the money in the ragbag, and the moaning in the attic were all but forgotten. Suddenly, it was school time again and time for revival at the church. We were settled into a new and prosperous way of life.

Mama and Grandma were members of the churchwomen's circle, which met on Saturday afternoons. It was there they gradually learned a little more about the Oates house and the people who had lived there. Mr. Oates had built the house several years after the War Between the States with his cotton profits; but as the years passed, things had seemed to fall apart for him. Cotton prices fell to where he could not make any money. He lost a child, a little girl, in the creek when torrential rains flooded the bottomland. One of his twin boys shot himself when he was sixteen, and that plus consumption killed Mrs. Oates. Less than a year later, Mr. Oates himself, beaten down by the world, died. They were all buried in the church cemetery. No one knew what happened to the remaining son. A man from Gaffney bought the property at a tax sale and sold off some of the land before reselling the property to Mr. Anderson, who let tenants have the place.

Mama in turn told the women's circle about the crash in the night out in the kitchen. The women oohed and aahed and said that the noise must have been made by the slave spirits that inhabited the house. There was a story that had been going around the community for quite a while about a number of household slaves who had been scalded to death in the kitchen of the Oates place when a large caldron of boiling water had turned over. The story explained some of the noises tenants had heard from time to time, and the women's circle agreed that our experience just confirmed it. If their conclusion was supposed to relieve our concerns, it did not. There was still some kind of a haint loose in our nice house. Besides, I later learned in school that the house hadn't even been built during slave times.

Even after the picking was done, fall was a busy time. After most of the cotton was sold, Daddy returned to the fields to plow under the weeds and cotton stalks. Mama was busy hanging onions and leather breeches and laying out apples and squash for winter storage in the root cellar. We children returned to school and, after we got home in the afternoons, helped however we could in the garden and fields as long as it was light enough outside. One day, Daddy and Mama took the wagon to the store; it was time to trade for some things we'd need for our second winter there. Grandma had a slight cold and decided to remain at home. She enjoyed sitting at the fireplace, reading her Bible, and occasionally dozing in the warmth when she caught up with her work.

It was early afternoon when she was aroused by the sound of rain – no, not the sound of rain; it was a drop of rain on her arm. It must have come a shower. She got up and was aware of a different sound coming from upstairs. It was not the horn, which immediately leapt to her mind, but the soft whir of a spinning wheel. Had the family gotten back while she was asleep? Was her daughter spinning some yarn? Where had she gotten wool? Where had she gotten the spinning wheel? We didn't have a spinning wheel! Grandma got up to investigate.

Finding no one in the lower part of the house, she headed toward the stairs. As she passed her rocking chair, her wrist suddenly felt wet. She looked down and saw something red on her hand. Startled, she stepped back and saw at her feet a small pool of red liquid, fresh and thick, on top of the old stains she had tried to scrub away last spring. She stood there for a moment, just staring at the red substance on her wrist, gradually realizing how much it looked like blood. Unexpectedly, she felt something brush by her, like a person passing her there in the room. She jumped back and let out a shriek. She hurriedly went to the front door, grabbing her shawl as she went, and left the house. She didn't take time to get her bonnet or parasol.

It was getting late and, although the rain had let up, the clouds made it dark for that time of day. Nevertheless, Grandma began walking rapidly toward the crossroads. About a quarter-mile down the road, she met Daddy and Mama and us children, whom they had picked up at school. She explained what happened. Back at home, Daddy saw the stain and knew what it looked like but opted to calm the situation.

"The roof is leaking," he said, pointing up to a faint circle on the ceiling boards.

He suggested that the rain had leaked into the loft and from there into the girls' room and down to the main floor. Grandma wouldn't have it. She puffed up, all 180 pounds of her, folded her arms, and said, "Harrumph! Since when does the rain come down red, Gat Dover?"

This time, Daddy had no answer. But he was determined to get to the bottom of this, for he had ten pairs of worried eyes looking at him. He announced that he'd not go into the loft that evening; it would not be possible to fix the leak while it was still raining. He'd get a ten-cent can of tar the next day at the store. Mama, Daddy, and Grandma then formed a group excluding the rest of us, and the group decided Daddy would go up and check out our bedroom. He took a bucket and a rag to get up the water he expected to find, despite the fact that it had never leaked in on us before.

When he came down a few minutes later, he was not talkative and seemed a little pale in the glow of the oil lamp. To be on the safe side and not get wet, we all got to pile into the bedroom downstairs, even the boys. We had two beds and a pile of pallets for the night.

First thing the next morning, Daddy hitched up Dob to the wagon and drove the five miles to our landlord's place. When Daddy got back, he gave us a short report of his conversation with Mr. Andrews. Andrews had been frank with Daddy.

"Gat, to be honest with you, yours is the first family that has stayed the entire season in that house since I bought it. I've always given a good deal to croppers like yourself, but none of them lasted more than a few months."

"Are you saying the place is hainted?"

"No, I'm not saying anything like that. But people died in the house, and some folks are nervous about staying in a house where somebody died."

Daddy told him he knew about the slaves scalding themselves and the boy killing himself but did not know any of the details. Mr. Andrews set him straight.

"There's never been any slaves there. The boy did hang himself out back, but they cut down the tree. And the woman killed herself in one of the rooms upstairs."

It seems that after she had found her son's body swinging from a tree, Mrs. Oates had lost her mind. She had caused her remaining son to run off to parts unknown; and, in her grief, she had taken the spindle off her spinning wheel and plunged it into her heart. Her husband had found her collapsed in an upstairs room – the same room in which my sisters and I slept – when he came in that evening. The blood had run all over the floor and dripped into the parlor.

When Daddy finished telling the whole story, Mama was silent. Grandma was ready to go that night, but Daddy persuaded her to wait until we'd found somewhere else to go. It took him just a week to arrange a move; Grandma had been in constant prayer for a new house, and it had worked. Daddy got us another farm not too many miles away at nearly the same terms. The new house was just a board cabin, smaller and cramped; but if anyone had ever died in it, they didn't think enough of it to stick around and haunt it.

Back then, we got our news by word of mouth, either at church or from the mailman. The mailman came by three times a week and always stopped a minute or two to get a dipper of cold well water and to speak to Daddy. It was late 1916 when he told Daddy about the Oates house burning down.

Sometime later, we heard that Mr. Anderson had hauled two hundred dollars' worth of lumber up to the place where the old house had stood. He planned to rebuild and hoped for better luck; but just after he had the new house framed up, it, too, caught fire. That made a lot of people think something was wrong with the whole Oates place, not just the old house. Mr. Anderson put cotton in himself, but he never did any good. Soon thereafter, the markets went crazy and war broke out; and sometime after the armistice, the boll weevils came, not long before Mr. Anderson died.

    I can't explain what happened during the time our family lived in the Oates house, nor why the place seemed cursed for a long time after; all I know for sure is, I was sure glad to leave it.

THE ONES WHO LIVED

Ghosts almost always are noticed because they take up residence in a house or other locale that was important to their living existence, a spot where they were comfortable or one in which some important aspect of their life played out. These spirits often remain for years as an established part of the environment, as much a fixture to be observed by passersby as cornice pieces on a roof or letters on a gravestone.

But there is another type of manifestation that is just as compelling, just as vivid as any that has long been widely reported, and that is the personal, private encounter with the paranormal. These more isolated hauntings are often experienced by a single individual; and whether they take place as a single event or a series of visitations, such occurrences can shake one's sense of reality because only he or she is affected. The individuals involved are often reluctant to admit it for fear of being thought crazy or otherwise unstable; and indeed, when such happenings do come to light, they are always questioned or dismissed by skeptics citing a number of possible explanations, from optical illusion to impaired perception. Thus, accounts such as these are rarely found in folklore and survive only in the oral tradition as second- or third-hand reports.

Two such accounts are discussed in this chapter. Both have been as well-documented as possible. The living individuals at the centers of these stories lived ordinary, productive lives both before and after their paranormal experiences. In the first case, the experience only lasted a matter of hours; in the second case, the visitation went on for weeks. Neither individual was physically harmed nor otherwise permanently afflicted, but both were profoundly affected thereafter. Both individuals were absolutely certain of what they saw and heard and felt.

Lisa lived well into her nineties. Although alone for the last thirty-odd years of her life, she remained cognizant of the world and able to care for herself almost to the end. Before the inevitable infirmities of age set in, she grew flowers and cultivated a small vegetable garden. Short and stocky with a resolute jaw, the tiny, bespectacled grandmother looked up at virtually everyone she met; nevertheless, with a firm and matronly voice that exuded confidence and honesty, she shared her opinions and advice freely.

Her certainty of truth was rooted in her faith and firmed by maturity; it never eroded. Perhaps she knew that she would accomplish something important in life, even if it was only raising half a dozen children to responsible adulthood and presenting them with her beliefs to accept or reject according to their choosing. She didn't force her children to attend church nor to follow in her spiritual footsteps; she just set the requisite example and encouraged correct behavior. She learned at an early age the main principle for her existence, and that was to live each day as if it were her last. That is where her story begins.

At the age of twelve, Lisa was living in Easley with her parents. That winter, she was stricken with influenza, the variety known as the Spanish Flu. It had followed in the wake of World War I, killing millions more than the war itself throughout Europe and Asia. It arrived in the United States in January of 1918 and spread rapidly through the cities and communities of the Upstate, lingering much longer than the usual course of the seasonal disease. It was especially prolific in the army camps in Greenville and Spartanburg. The disease could strike a person ill in the morning and kill that person before dark. In the era before antibiotics, it was the deadliest form of influenza that most of the world had ever seen.

The bedridden Lisa remained listless and barely responsive. Her fever soared and persisted. When the doctor finally came, he took a look, checked the child's heart and temperature, and readied her mother for the worst. He explained that the fever was the body's way of burning out the disease but that it weakened Lisa while it was fighting the illness.

"Unless this fever breaks pretty soon," he said, "Lisa is probably going to die."

The doctor told Lisa's mother that her daughter might go into a coma, as he had seen others do; it might be easier that way. She would just go to sleep and never wake up. In the meantime, he had to run; there were scores of new cases to which he had to attend, and he might be able to help some of them. He would be back to check on Lisa when he could, but there was nothing else he could do at present.

At the door, the doctor turned to warn the mother, "The fever is like a double-edged axe; it cuts both ways. If it gets too high and lasts too long, well… Watch her. Keep her comfortable. Cool her down if she gets too hot; you'll know it when you see it." His voice trailed off as he walked to the street.

Hours later, when the child began to sweat, Lisa's mother silently rejoiced. Lisa was still fighting. Throughout the next two days, the child had fits of restlessness, never coming fully awake, interspersed among periods of stillness in which her breathing became almost imperceptible. Her mother applied cold compresses and wiped Lisa's face and arms with wet washcloths. She never stopped talking to Lisa and almost never left the bedside.

It was over in the second night when Lisa awoke to full consciousness for the first time since the onset of her illness. She was still hot and flung the blanket off her body, but she was no longer sweating. She lay on the sheet dressed just in her nightgown. In the dim yellow glow from the oil lamp on the dresser, Lisa could make out her mother's sleeping form in the armchair that had been pulled close to the bed. Lisa called weakly for her mother, but the exhausted woman was too deeply asleep to hear the small voice. Every part of Lisa's body felt too heavy; she was thirsty but could barely move her arms, much less get them to the pitcher on the table by the bed.

Feeling a draft, Lisa turned her head toward the door at the end of the parlor across the hall. It opened further, admitting a cool, refreshing breeze that gave her relief. From out of the darkness stepped a woman, a woman who looked familiar. Lisa gave no thought to the fact that it was near two o'clock in the morning when in walked her great-aunt, her mother's Aunt Millie. Wearing a yellow dress so bright that it almost glowed, Aunt Millie seemed to illuminate the room. Without speaking, she sat down on the edge of the bed and began stroking the child's hair with one hand. The soft touch of her aunt's hand was pleasant and reassuring. Lisa relaxed in the coolness and drifted in and out of sleep the rest of the night. Each time she awoke, there was Aunt Millie, smiling down at her.

There was no conversation between them that Lisa ever remembered, but it was as if she knew what Aunt Millie was thinking: "You need more rest. Go back to sleep now."

Lisa asked, or maybe just thought, "Are you going to wake Mama?" In reply, Aunt Millie just smiled ever so pleasantly, then leaned to kiss the child on the forehead. She gently touched her grandniece's hand once more before rising and exiting the way she came in, leaving the door open. The draft from the open door soothed Lisa as it cooled her. She drifted off to sleep again.

When she awoke again, it was morning; the sun was shining, sending soft rays of light between the parted curtains. She glanced over at her mother, still asleep in the chair but wrapped in the blanket Elizabeth had flung off. Lisa felt weak as a kitten but fully conscious and, for the first time in days, cold. The house was cool; the fire had died during the night. The door was closed. Only the barely burning lamp gave off warmth. Now capable of movement, Lisa adjusted herself in bed. The sounds of rustling bed covers awakened her mother, who still looked tired. A smile spread across her mother's face when she felt Lisa's head and found it cool.

Lisa asked, "Where is Aunt Millie?"

Her mother narrowed her eyes questioningly but said nothing. Lisa continued, "Aunt Millie came last night."

"It must have been a dream," said her mother. "Aunt Millie lives in Charlotte. That's nearly a hundred miles from here. I'm glad you slept and dreamed; you were so restless until your fever broke."

Lisa's mother had only the vaguest memory of getting up, checking Lisa's head for fever, and closing the door that must have blown open in the early morning hours. When Lisa's appetite returned, her mother prepared some potato soup and fed her slowly. Just as Lisa finished her meal, a knock came at the door. The boy from the depot had brought a telegram for her mother. Her mother took the note and began reading but then suddenly paled and dropped her hand. Alarmed, Lisa asked what was the matter. Her mother sat down, and tears began to stream from her surprised eyes.

"Uncle Harry," she said, "sent this telegram to let us know that Aunt Millie passed away during the night. She had the flu, too, and seemed to be about over it; but she took a turn for the worse after midnight, and nothing could be done."

Lisa never again saw her great-aunt's spirit, but that night's visit indelibly marked her memory. She certainly did not share her experience with everyone she met, but her family knew about it, as did her most trusted friends. She never recanted the story nor varied in the details for the next seventy-five years of her life, always convincing and always convinced that she had spent precious time in the presence of her aunt.

Interesting stories of the Roaring Twenties are usually set in the big cities, such as Chicago, New York, Atlanta, Charleston, and New Orleans; but the Twenties brought change in public values and attitudes to virtually every nook and cranny in America. The Great War was over, and prosperity was around the corner for those who worked hard. Inventive Americans were manufacturing new consumer goods that even the average household could afford to make life easier and more enjoyable. It was the era of the automobile, the washing machine, and the radio. Planes flew in the skies; cars replaced the horse and buggy. Progress could not be held back.

Social attitudes were also in flux. Skirts shortened, and music sped up; smoking and drinking, particularly by women in public places, marked the coming-of-age of a new generation. Couples met without chaperones; clubs and honky-tonks proliferated. New sets of societal mores were set to replace pre-war conservatism in a mad rush into the Twentieth Century.

With progress comes growing pains. Not every village and hamlet readily accepted what was viewed by some as encroaching evil. In the small town of Greer, increasing use of alcohol became the main problem for law enforcement after the war and well into the 1920s, despite prohibition laws. Although legally dry since 1879, Greer had had its share of heartache originating from the misuse of alcohol. The law did little to deter bootleggers from bringing liquor into town for sale. Small cafes and dives in and outside the town limits served as blind tigers where hooch was available under the counter. Cheap and convenient booze fueled a crime wave in Greer that led to a revamping of the police department.

Chief of Police Dave Moore, selected in 1922, found himself bound by difficulties from the start. The department was undermanned and its resources spread thin trying to deal with the many crimes originating on the outskirts of town. Petty crime remained rife, and scandal rocked Greer for months when a prostitute named Dorothy Dodson died under mysterious circumstances just outside the town limits in October of 1924. The finer points of jurisdiction and manpower notwithstanding,

Chief Moore lost the confidence of the city fathers and was replaced in early 1925.

W. J. Tapp, age fifty-two, manager of the company store at Apalache Mill, applied to the town council for the job of police chief. His wife of thirty years, Corrie, and his church brethren supported him in his bid. Too much of a Christian to speak ill of the man who had held the job previously, Tapp instead said that the leaders should demand a higher standard of enforcement and equal treatment of all citizens under the law. In his application, he promised to bring all the grief caused by liquor to an end, not considering that he would be saddled with basically the same set of limitations that had faced his predecessor: a small force of men, limited jurisdiction, lack of a city vehicle, and a growing population. Although he had little, if any, actual law enforcement experience, Tapp was confident that a firm hand and fair treatment, the means by which he had administered authority in his previous job, would be effective in keeping his promise.

Tapp, a man of strong moral fiber and community connections, got the job. He accepted with the condition that the police department be reorganized. The council agreed, and before Tapp took the job, all but one of the three previous officers had been replaced. The council hired S. O. Mahaffey as a special officer and rehired W. L. Flynn as a temporary officer.

Despite high hopes for the new police department, things seemed to go from bad to worse. A prisoner committed suicide while in police custody. Professional burglars struck a local dry goods store and escaped with a thousand dollars, a small fortune at the time. A young girl was kidnapped, and another murder occurred just outside of Tapp's jurisdiction, which nevertheless called attention to just how helpless the town was in dealing with crime, especially on its periphery. Chief Tapp worked with the

Greenville and Spartanburg County authorities and the mill deputy at Victor to try to clear some cases; but the backlog was great, and many of the petty criminals simply got away with their acts by moving out of legal reach.

The Dorothy Dodson case, which had been the bane of Chief Moore's term of office, continued to fuel sermons by local ministers for a year. The preacher at the Baptist church, Reverend Porter Marcellus Bailes, whom some canonized as "the conscience of Greer," compared the town with Chicago as a den of iniquity and evil.

It must be understood that Tapp and his men made plenty of arrests but mostly for petty crimes such as drunkenness and larceny. The crimes that made the papers and were most publicly discussed were the ones for which Tapp and his men were unable to prepare or, because of jurisdiction, unable to pursue. Well into his second year in office, Chief Tapp had been unable to make any obvious headway against crime in Greer. Despite Tapp's limited success, the city council stood by the chief.

Tapp's ancestors had been farmers, so he understood well the old saying, "Do what you can with what you have." There was a limit to where he could assign his men and how many cases they could handle at one time. The chief's predecessors had all taken a day or two off each week and worked the night shift. To demonstrate his concern and sense of fairness, Tapp was on the job seven days a week and still took his turn along with his men on the night shift. His dedication to the job impressed Greer's citizens and its council; and eventually, the town limits became virtually free of even minor mischief.

Chief Tapp was on duty one evening in 1927 when a call came in from a café on the east side of town. East Greer was composed of a few tiny store buildings on Arlington Road, some operating as businesses and others serving to house hobos or squatters. At the café, a patron had been drinking and had reached the point at which he was mean and threatening. He had run off all the other customers with threats and physical abuse. The owner was afraid.

Tapp drove his own car to the café. When he arrived, he found only the owner behind the counter at the front and the drunken patron sitting at a table in the rear of the building with his head down. The building was three times as long as it was wide, with a counter, scattered tables and chairs, and a small kitchen in the back. A plate glass window in front provided most of the lighting; the rest came from two lightbulbs suspended from the ceiling on long cords of electrical wire.

The chief walked in, acknowledged the proprietor, and assessed the situation. He directed a few comments to the man at the table. The man responded by mumbling, "I'm going to cut me somebody."

The man sat facing the chief with one arm hanging by his side. After making his announcement, he stood unsteadily and then raised his hand to reveal an open pocketknife. He was a big man, with eyes wide and intent as he began moving from behind the table toward the front of the building; the chief was twenty or so feet away.

The chief was not wearing a gun belt, as it was not his habit. The uniform of the day was a business suit, but the chief often dropped a revolver into his jacket pocket anytime he thought it might be a good idea. This was one of those times. He felt the heaviness of the gun through the fabric as he watched the man in the back of the room move closer. The man's eyes were red and wild; he walked more steadily after a few steps, holding the knife out in front of him.

Chief Tapp warned the man to drop the knife and stand still, but the order was ignored. There were no tables between the two men now as the one continued to advance. When it became clear the man was going to use the knife in his hand, the chief pulled his revolver and fired a single shot. The bullet passed through the man, whose eyes registered the shock of disbelief. He stood motionless for what seemed to be forever before slowly dropping his head to watch blood stream from the hole in his shirt where a dark stain was widening. He stumbled back toward the table, fumbling for support before finally finding the chair and slipping down into it. His eyes affixed on the chief, who had not moved, and they remained on the chief as they became glassy in death.

The chief called the station and asked that other officers get there as soon as possible. He then called the coroner, who came and took the statement of the only witness in the room. The chief sat at a table until the body was removed. The dead man's name was Adam Watson; he had never gotten in trouble before to anyone's knowledge.

The shooting was justified as self-defense, and for most citizens, that was the final word. For the chief, this was just the beginning. The shock of what had happened numbed him for a few days, and then he began to think more about the event. The verdict of self-defense did not grant the chief the peace of mind that he longed for. When he went to bed at night, he slept little; every time he closed his own eyes, he saw the open, red eyes of the dying man, shocked and amazed at his own death.

Tapp told his best friend, Broughton Colvin, a tire dealer and volunteer fireman, that he couldn't get those eyes out of his mind. Deprived of rest, the chief became shaky and nervous; he lost weight and became physically ill. He experienced symptoms that could not be tied to a single disease. He became restless but could not walk well. On the verge of some kind of physical collapse, the chief offered his resignation to the city council "for reasons of health," keeping the real reason to himself. The council refused and told him to take a few days off. He agreed to do so; but the days off stretched into weeks. Instead of finding solace in his time for reflection, Tapp only found increasing torment.

He began to see the dead man's form inside his own home. Each night when the lights were turned off, he could make out the form of the man in the corner of the room, just standing and watching him with those wild red eyes. He grabbed his handgun the first time and leaped from bed to turn on a light only to see the furnishings of the room as they should be and no sign of what had been so vivid when he opened his eyes in darkness. Another time, he awakened his wife so she might see for herself, but she never saw anything. After some rough nights, she moved into another room to get some rest. When the chief finally managed to get some sleep, it was brief and fitful; he would jerk into wakefulness from the least noise, even an imagined noise, and shine his flashlight into the recesses of the room.

What few moments of sleep he could get were haunted by nightmares. The dying man invaded the chief's every dream night after night. Upon waking, he experienced the memory of the dreams as vividly as the dreams themselves. Those who were close to the chief pitied him for his obvious decline, although they had no clue what he was going through.

At the recommendation of his doctor, the town council gave Tapp an indefinite leave of absence. He was temporarily replaced by the chief of the volunteer fire department, S. O. Mahaffey. Things did not get better, and after nearly a month off duty, Tapp again offered his resignation to the council and again was refused. The council was impressed by the chief's courage; rumors had sprung up about him standing up to a knife-wielding criminal and shooting him dead, which had had a deterring effect on local crime. The chief was told to return when he wanted to and on whatever terms would work for him.

Relieved of any pressure to return to full-time duty, Tapp gradually came to terms with his experience and returned to work. Eventually, he was able to carry out all of his duties on the rigorous schedule he had set for himself when he first came to the job. He told Colvin that he no longer saw the spirit of the man he killed. The dreams had subsided. The memories of that night remained with him for the rest of his life, but he was able to keep them from interfering with his life and work. He told those who inquired about his health and wellbeing that he was feeling better, that his ailments had improved. He did not go into any detail about his experiences except to Colvin.

Tapp served as chief of police until he reached retirement age. He worked as hard at the end as he had when he started out; he considered his eighty-four-hour workweek worth the $1,450 annual salary it brought. By 1940, he was something of a local legend. He had done what he set out to do fifteen years earlier – within the town limits, the law was respected, as were the officers who enforced it. Serious crime had been reduced, partly as a result of greater attention by county officers of both Greenville and Spartanburg.

Tapp continued to confide in his friend Broughton Colvin as long as he lived. When Tapp got on the subject of those nights after the shooting, he consistently maintained that the man was actually there; the ghost, demon, or whatever you might call him had been in the bedroom, on the streets, in the alley, and wherever the chief had found himself alone, as real as anyone he ever talked to on the street in the daytime. Colvin did not belabor the subject, but some years later, he asked his friend what had happened to the apparition. Tapp told him, "Nothing happened to that man; whatever happened, happened to me."

Tapp went on to explain that he had never doubted the necessity of doing what he had done; legally, he was in the clear and his life had been threatened. But in the act of taking a life, some edge of his personality had been dulled. He had gained more depth, a greater sense of doubt and concern. He had never planned for anything like that to happen, and he never wanted it to happen again, either to himself or to any of his men. Colvin remembered that each time he and Tapp had these talks, the chief always second-guessed himself: "Maybe I was too fast; maybe I could have waited; maybe I should have waited."

And often he would say these words while looking off into the distance, as though he were speaking to someone else.

RETURN OF THE HATCHET MAN

It was late summer, 1952, when the deputies who still wore dark suits instead of uniforms came to the house. They pulled up in the driveway in a black 1950 Ford Coach late in the day; the sun was already behind the hill beyond the trees. The boy and his parents had been about to sit down for supper when the headlights flashed through the window and the tires crunched over freshly scattered cinders in the driveway. The boy followed his daddy to the porch and stayed, half-hidden, behind his daddy's leg, but the big men with serious faces had no time for little boys. They might have been friends of his daddy, except that the grayest one called his daddy "Mister."

The other thing that told the little boy that the men were not his daddy's friends was the badge that peeked out from under one man's coat as he hooked one forefinger under his lapel and gestured toward the river a quarter-mile away.

"Somebody found a dead man on the side of the road near Miller Bridge. We think he was a Negro. The driver who reported it said he didn't stop; he slowed enough to see that it was a person who looked dead but couldn't tell much else. The body was lying mostly in the grass, with one part, maybe a foot, protruding out into the road. The driver almost ran over it. One of the magistrate's constables – either Green or Howell, don't remember which – went to check it out, but when he got there, there was nothing to be found. We're looking further into the matter to find out what is going on.

"Mr. Meadows said you found some blood on your porch steps?" It was more of a question than a statement as the deputy tried to confirm the discovery, but the officer was disappointed.

"Hell, no, I haven't found any blood or anything else that shouldn't be on my place. Bud Meadows, is that who you're talking about? He can't tell something or 'nother from a hole in the ground. To think anybody in the country would believe a word that flew out of Bud Meadows' mouth! Everybody knows he is unreliable." The boy's daddy caught himself before he lost too much of his Sunday School speaking; he stopped and looked down, silently fuming while the deputy apologized.

The boy's daddy fumbled around in his shirt pocket, extracted a Camel from a half-empty pack, tapped it against the wall, and placed it in between his lips. He then held the pack toward the deputies, but they both shook their heads. He struck a match, applied it to the tip, inhaled, and blew smoke toward the door; he still had not spoken another word. After another moment or two, he continued his end of the conversation; he finished setting the deputies straight about Bud Meadows and then offered to help them if he heard anything.

The deputies apologized again for bothering him and, after a round of handshaking and final observations about the dry weather, the men settled back into their Ford and backed out of the yard. Before they pulled away, the boy's daddy stepped to the edge of the road and told the deputies to see Henry Wilson, owner of the local sand pump, if they needed a report on any blood. Ten years older than the boy's daddy, Henry could track a pig over concrete and spot a deer flagging half a mile away. The deputies didn't know Henry but thought he sounded like he might be of some help.

That night, as the family sat eating the usual Tuesday fare of cornbread and black-eyed peas, the boy's daddy casually mentioned, perhaps in an effort to ease some of the tension from earlier, that the Hatchet Man may have gotten the body on the road.

"Who?" asked the boy.

His mama looked mean at her husband and told him in no uncertain terms not to scare the boy. "He'll start peeing on the bed again if you get him upset."

Despite the boy's curiosity, nothing more was said at the supper table about the Hatchet Man, so it was up to the boy to find out from other sources who the Hatchet Man was. Besides, he hadn't wet the bed in weeks and probably never would again in his life!

The boy lived with his parents in a four-room frame house on a mostly empty road, having escaped the crowded mill village just two years earlier. Their closest neighbors, the Martins, who lived a good hundred yards distant down a long driveway out of sight from the road, had three kids, but they were all much older than the boy; the two daughters were in school and the son was in service. The Fletcher sisters lived out past where the road disappeared around a curve. They were old, that's all the boy knew. And then there was Aunt Lilly, the boy's closest adult associate.

Lilly Webb had been a widow since the late '30s and pretty close to blind since the end of the war, but she lived alone because she could. She regularly cooked, washed clothes in cold water, and hit the house a lick with a broom. Her children were grown and gone. Alone most of the time, she agreed to let the boy come to her house after school each day to stay until his parents came from the mill over in town where they worked, where they would always work. After the first few weeks, the boy became a sort of honorary grandchild. Lilly would often tell his parents that he was a big help.

Besides her blindness, Aunt Lilly suffered other infirmities. She was elderly, obese, and arthritic, and she had a tiny cancer on her lower gum (which she would not find out about until the boy was a grown man and she was very old). Some might think such a person ill-suited to watch after an eight-year-old boy, but she kept him occupied with small tasks, such as getting towels off the shelf, or finding her snuff, or fetching her spit can. If he misbehaved, Aunt Lilly would reach over the side of her chair and scratch the upholstery pretty hard, telling the boy it was the old booger man trying to get in the window.

When he wasn't doing chores, the boy was sitting by Lilly's side, captivated by a range of stories running the gamut from her childhood memories of riding her daddy's mule around the cane mill to accounts of shootings and other crimes that had been the news of the day during her long lifetime. When it came to his question about Hatchet Man, Aunt Lilly was reluctant to go into detail. She simply said she didn't remember much about it; it had been a long time ago, and would he go and get her a handkerchief out of the drawer, the one with the yellow flowers on it. As if it mattered!

The boy got a little more information from Lois the next Saturday. Lois was a young black woman who did housework for some of the white people in the area. She lived with her husband in a concrete blockhouse at the bottom of the hill below the slaughterhouse on Miller Road. The boy's mama got Lois to do the laundry on Saturdays and to watch the boy if the mill was running six days that week.

Lois fixed his dinner of fried potatoes, cornbread, and some leftover creamed corn, and then sat down to rest a few minutes. The boy brought up the subject that was on his mind. Lois got quiet and looked out the open door in the direction of the road before speaking.

"The old people used to say he's a spirit who gets bad people. That's what the old people say."

The boy was wide-eyed as he ate the piece of cornbread covered in syrup that Lois had put on his plate. She poured herself a glass of tea and then told him the basics, as her mama had told her.

"Mama said he wasn't no ghost but a real man, name of Furman Brown. He worked for Mr. Jackson up on Ansel Road before my mama was even born. He took sick – got to where he couldn't talk or walk for the longest time – but then got better. But he lost his mind when he got back on his feet. Mama said he went plumb crazy. People said he got to where he didn't know his wife or children. When that happened the last time, he took a hatchet and chopped them to pieces one morning after breakfast.

"Mr. Jackson found them when he went to see why Furman hadn't come to work. It was up in the morning, and he was just sitting in there amongst the dead, all bloody and wild-looking. He pushed by Mr. Jackson and took to the big woods that stretched from down behind Jackson's house back on down the hill to the river and all the way to the millpond.

"Mr. Jackson sent for the law, but Furman had just vanished. They looked for two or three days, all up and down the river, dragging the pond and everything. They never found him."

The following Monday after school, the boy shared a little of what Lois had told him with Aunt Lilly, who then decided to set the boy straight. Lois had got some of it wrong and left other parts out. Back when they were first searching for Brown, deputies had found tracks at the river, but the tracks hadn't gone anywhere. The deputies had thought Brown might have tried to get across and maybe drowned, since nobody up nor downstream had reported seeing him on foot. Lilly didn't remember anything about them dragging the pond. People living on the mill village way on downstream had been notified to look out for the body, since it might surface on the millpond and float awhile, but it never did.

Some people figured he had gotten away. Others believed he had died in the river and his bones were at the bottom of the millpond. The new sheriff had promised in his campaign that he would reopen some of the unsolved cases his opponent had given up on, but that never happened. It had made the city papers briefly and then had been dropped for more interesting news; after all, someone was killed every Saturday night at one honky-tonk or another. But out in the country, the legend had grown.

For years, every time something strange happened in that section, it had been blamed on old Furman Brown, whom they came to call Hatchet Man. Chickens had been stolen, clothes had been taken off clotheslines, dogs had been killed, strangers had been seen lurking at a distance just out of focus – any of these things could reasonably point to the continued presence of Hatchet Man in the community.

Toward the end of the 1920s, when old Lacy Warden disappeared, people had started carrying guns wherever they went, including to the outhouse. This had gone on for weeks until a hunter had found Lacy at the edge of a dove field where he had frozen to death, drunk. He had curled up like a baby for warmth, as natural as could be. Frozen he was, but that was just according to the coroner; people had kept their opinions about it.

Now that a body had been reported and disappeared, a new round of Hatchet Man sightings was due. Sure enough, the next Monday at school, even the third graders had heard about some old woman who lived on Miller Road having seen him. He had run through the headlights of her old '47 Chevrolet as she came home from church. Mrs. Burnett was old but reliable enough that some men, neighbors, came to her house and looked around Sunday night until they were satisfied Hatchet Man was gone – if he had been there at all.

The community went on alert; for a while, men carried whatever they had in the way of weapons with them when they went to feed chickens, milk cows, put out hay, crank their cars, or check their mailboxes. Hitchhikers were completely out of luck for several weeks. Women hung their wash on racks in their houses, and several discussions at church centered around mysterious noises heard in the night, as if someone were tossing small rocks on a porch or against the side of a house to get inhabitants to come out in the dark.

Although the weeks passed without either victim or perpetrator turning up, the latest Hatchet Man scare became delicious fodder for Halloween consumption. Reports of sightings increased, but no one seemed to be able to find an eyewitness. Officers gave up their investigation the week following the report of a body, but the community didn't seem to want to let go of the matter quite so readily.

October 31 was a holiday to be enjoyed by both young and old, especially when the local PTA chapter hosted their annual Halloween carnival fundraiser. There was a fish pond, a cake walk, a movie room that showed Abbot and Costello meeting one monster or another, a "spook room" where people wearing false-faces impersonated spirits, and exhibits of students' work. Teachers were on hand to talk to parents. Local stores contributed door prizes, and firecrackers boomed for hours, beginning before sunset. That year, attendance was up and fairly rife with young Hatchet Man impersonators who had rummaged through old clothes to achieve the proper effect.

That fall had been a turning point toward manhood for the boy. He still had a long way to go, but he had observed his daddy and the other people around him and learned about something that he would not have been grown up enough to know about before. Despite his mother's prediction, the boy's new store of knowledge had not caused a relapse of bed-wetting. In fact, believing he knew more than his classmates about certain aspects of the tale caused the boy to feel good about himself, as good as he would for a long time to come.

Suddenly, it was November. The air turned chill, and the boy began working daily on a Thanksgiving poster for the class bulletin board. One Monday after school, he headed for the Martin house; Aunt Lilly was in Raleigh for a week, visiting her last sibling. The boy was allowed to play alone outside at the Martins', since he had little in common with the teenage girls other than being a member of the same species.

The sky was beginning to purple when he wandered to the barn at the edge of the woods. The big door was open. There were no animals left; Mr. Martin had sold his horse the year before, and the cow had gone with her calf earlier that year when feed got too high and the family found store-bought milk to be just as sweet.

Just inside the barn door and to the right was a little room where Mr. Martin had his small workshop. The door was closed, but nobody had told the boy not to go in there, so he did. It smelled funny, not like the fragrant mixture of manures and sweet feed; it reminded him of... peanut butter? And was that a rat he heard bump a tin can on the floor? As his eyes adjusted to the dimness, he turned at the sound to see a pair of legs; he followed them up a slender frame to stare into a pair of terrible eyes. In the dusty shadows behind the door stood a thin, gray-bearded black man in a ragged suit coat and tattered felt hat; and held prominently against his chest was a bloody hatchet.

Late that night, even in the safety and comfort of his own bed in his own home with both his parents there to console and protect him, the boy still shivered with fear. He had been told that the specter in the barn was just Brian Martin, AWOL from Donaldson Air Base and trying to elude the MPs, yet he still searched for a way to fix Hatchet Man into the proper niche of his childhood memory. Thirty years later, with the warm body of his wife lying beside him and his own boy asleep in the next room in their home, three states away from his childhood, there were still times that the boy-become-man would jerk awake and blink to convince himself it had only been a dream.

Had somebody actually seen a body on the roadside? What were the kernels of truth contained in the Hatchet Man tales? All the adults at least gave lip service to disbelief in "any such haints," but the rumors persisted, perhaps too captivating to let go. By the end of that season, even the most casehardened skeptics in the neighborhood started locking their doors at night, for there were other dangers out there, real outlaws and no-accounts running loose in the night. And all the Halloweens that followed were never again quite so innocent.

THE ORGANIST OF LIBERTY

The Liberty church sat in a quiet grove north of town, protected on three sides by large oaks and bounded by a road that was infrequently traveled. It was of modest size with modest attendance, although it had on its active rolls the names of well over a hundred souls. Its cemetery held tombstones bearing dates as early as the 1700s.

The parsonage was located a hundred feet from the sanctuary. A small social hall sat immediately to the rear of the educational wing. The nearest house was located a few hundred yards down the road and was not visible from church nor parsonage. Other neighbors were few and far between.

No industry operated in the church's vicinity; this was farm country. The only enterprise in the area in recent years had been a sawmill that had come and gone eight or ten years earlier. Only the dirt road and a massive pile of rotting sawdust at the end of it marked the fact that industrial noises of trucks and machinery had ever spoiled the tranquility of the countryside.

The day set for the new preacher's arrival was a chilly Thursday in early December. It was not the typical time for the changing of the guard in a church, the date falling between two holidays, but it was the most convenient for those in transition. The weather had been good and promised a few more nice but chilly days in the foreseeable future. The preacher and his wife were driving along with the movers to guide them to the new house; but due to unforeseen circumstances, the movers had been delayed several hours. It would be near dark before the van would arrive.

The minister's son and son-in-law each drove an hour after he got off work to come and help with the move; in the days before mobile phones, they had no way of knowing about the movers' delay. They both arrived a little after four o'clock in the fading light of the afternoon, the son arriving first by ten minutes or so. The house was locked, and no one else was around, so the young man decided to explore the church building and grounds.

Arriving a few minutes later, the son-in-law and his expectant wife, who had come along as a surprise to her parents, saw that her brother Don had already gotten there. Don's car was in the parsonage driveway, but Don himself was nowhere to be seen. The couple checked the house and, finding it locked, decided to take a look at the church; this was the first time they had ever seen it.

When they got to the front of the church, they heard the faint, belabored, almost scratchy notes of an organ being played. They assumed Don was at the keyboard. He was a musician of some talent and, although his instrument was the guitar, he probably couldn't resist the keyboard if he was killing time.

They tried the front door of the church but found it locked; they knocked but received no answer. Maybe Don couldn't hear them for his playing. They found a side entrance, but it, too, was locked. At the rear of the building, at the bottom of a set of cement stairs, they found a basement door that was also secure.

The music continued as they finished circumnavigating the building and stopped just before they met Don on the sidewalk out front; he said he had been just ahead of them, shaking the doors himself.

Don's sister asked why he hadn't let them in. He told her that he had not been inside the church.

"Well, who was playing the organ?" she asked.

"I heard that, too. Must have been someone from the church," he replied.

About that time, the moving van rolled into the driveway, and the driver maneuvered it into unloading position. Two men jumped out and rapidly began preparing for their work. It wasn't until almost eleven that the lights of the van disappeared around the bend in the road. A few members of the church, who had come by with food for the family, shook hands with the new preacher and departed. While the young men sipped coffee in preparation for their drive back, the family had a little time to discuss their long, busy day.

The movers' delay had come about because of a breakdown, and more time was lost because of traffic. Other than that, the day had gone pretty well. The minister asked the young folks how they liked the church.

"Well, the outside looks pretty substantial," answered the son-in-law. He went on to explain that they were going to look inside but had found the doors locked, as they should be. As the young folks compared notes, they realized they still could not account for the music. The welcome party from the church had not come until well after the moving van had arrived, and no one else had been around.

They discussed the possibility of a neighbor's radio but dismissed that when they learned how far away the nearest neighbor was. Could it have been a clock's chimes, maybe one of those with the Westminster bells? No, they agreed the sound was definitely a hymn, although they couldn't agree which one it was. Don believed it was "Nearer My God To Thee," while his sister believed it was "How Great Thou Art." They were in the midst of head-scratching when they remembered the next day was a work day for the young men and rose to go.

The preacher was up early the next day despite the late night before. It was Friday, and he had a sermon to get ready in two days. He moved just enough of his notes, files, and books into the small study beside the church office to get started. It was cozy and warm, if a little cramped. He prepared his first sermon in the silence of the study while his wife arranged doodads and knickknacks in the closets and cabinets and shelves of their new home. There would, no doubt, be visitors from the congregation coming by soon; and, of course, the reverend and missus had to be ready to answer the needs of any member as best they could at any time.

Sunday arrived, and the preacher's inaugural sermon was well-received. His son and daughter and son-in-law were there for this new beginning. It might be awhile before the daughter could return, for her delivery time was rapidly approaching.

The weeks flew by as the preacher and his wife settled into their new home. During the weekdays, they rarely saw anyone except seventy-year-old Sam Crisp, the part-time janitor, who came in Friday mornings to put in half a day cleaning the sanctuary and restrooms. If he didn't finish, he would come back Saturday. He also arrived early every Sunday morning to get the furnace going during cold weather. He'd always yell down the hall toward the study as he went to begin his labors, and the preacher, if there, would yell a friendly greeting back.

When he wasn't visiting members, the preacher could usually be found ensconced in his study, seated comfortably in the high-backed rolling chair before a sprawling oak desk that took up much of the floor space. There, he found it easy to concentrate deeply on sermon topics. Sometimes he would be so engrossed in finessing a point that he would jump when a stray sound suddenly broke his concentration.

At first, he didn't think much about it. Old buildings make noises. It was just the popping and cracking of the timber frame expanding and contracting with changes in the weather; and if it wasn't that, it was the sound coming from the furnace pipes responding to the same natural forces. But after some weeks at the new church, the minister found himself sometimes paying more attention to the noises than to his sermons.

He asked his wife one afternoon when he came home for lunch if she had come to the church for something earlier. She responded that she had not. She had been busy with the ironing all morning and afterwards had put together the apple pie that he was about to enjoy for dessert.

"Why?" she asked.

"Well, I could be wrong, but I thought I heard the door open and close."

"You must have been mistaken. Maybe it was Sam."

When it happened again some days later, the preacher heard the unmistakable soft squeaks of hardwood boards under carpet, like someone walking down the aisle. Thinking it might be one of his members, he got up to greet his visitor, stepped out of the study, and saw... no one. He walked to the front door, stepped outside to check the parking area, and found it vacant as usual. At supper, he casually informed his wife that he could have erred again and gave her the details. This time, she had nothing to say on the subject.

By the time his first grandchild arrived, the minister had gotten to know his congregation and some of the larger community pretty well. He had visited half the active members in their homes, had seen two in the local hospital, and had met three more in two nursing homes. He had met with store managers, teachers, and deputies, each of whom he invited to visit the church. He had learned about local history, traditions, and current events on the minds of locals. He had also picked up plenty of gossip as he acquainted himself with the community.

He was cautioned by one farmer about a bunch of stray dogs that roamed nearby and occasionally killed chickens. The farmer and some of his neighbors had killed off a few of the dogs, but more still hung around the old sawmill. A woman, whose name the farmer would not utter for fear of slander (although he did share that she drove a Lincoln Town Car and was as eccentric as one could imagine), was in the habit of buying scrap cuts of meat and feeding the dogs. She thought she was being kind, but the farmer thought it unwise. Something bad was going to come of it; but there was no law broken and nothing that could be done about it, since it was her land and her money.

The preacher learned about plenty of other small differences between neighbors and some of the inevitable but hopefully slight frictions between various members of his church. They all reminded him of a Bible teacher at college who had once told the class, "You will always find disagreements when you have a crowd of two or more people."

Although he was never directly asked about it, more than once did the minister hear rumors of the ghost. He was not a believer in ghosts of any description; in his opinion, it was not doctrinal to believe that way. But he was interested in learning what people had to say if for no other reason than to be a more effective shepherd. Finally, he chose to broach the subject with an educated, highly respected former deacon.

The old deacon revealed to him that some folks believed they had seen the spirit of a Confederate soldier, whose remains were buried in the churchyard, inside the church itself. The old deacon had never seen anything himself, but he continued with a litany of reports of strange goings-on that supposedly had been experienced by others whom he declined to identify.

Those who found themselves alone in the church sometimes heard sounds well in excess of what one would expect from a settling structure. The sounds were described as footsteps, coughing, and sometimes music that seemed to echo within the otherwise empty church. The minister did not mention that he had some of his own thoughts about the noises in the church, nor did he say anything about his children's experience. He kept the conversation at an academic, hypothetical level.

One member was adamant that he had heard the organ playing by itself, but the deacon had had to dismiss that claim, because the old pump organ bellows was busted. The instrument had long ago seen its better days, and the only reason it was still occupying its niche was that the father of a certain prominent lady had donated the thing to the church seventy-five years ago.

The preacher took his accumulating mass of information with him and tried to assimilate it into his philosophy. He was not afraid. He took his Bible and went to his study with as much courage as any man. He placed a radio in the study, selected a station that carried religious programming, and played it at a low volume to cancel out any unusually loud settling of the building. This worked within reason, except that for two hours each day he had to learn to tolerate sermons that reflected the doctrines of a rival denomination.

Spring arrived, and the minister and his wife put in a small vegetable garden. During the warm months, the couple spent many pleasant afternoons outside. Summer and fall saw a good harvest of fresh vegetables; Christmas came and went, and their first grandchild celebrated a birthday. The congregation liked their new preacher, he and his wife enjoyed their labors and their new friends, and the first year passed happily.

The pastor did most of his studies during the day; but as preparations began for the spring revival, he found himself falling behind. He remained after prayer meeting one Wednesday night to jot down some new ideas that had struck him as particularly useful. His wife had already gone home, saying her goodnights and walking out with the crowd.

Coming out of his study sometime later, the preacher took time to close the door and make sure the light was switched off. As he walked up the aisle in the dim rays of the vestibule light, the pastor heard something that sounded vaguely musical. Turning toward the front of the church, he peered into the darkness of the niche where the old pump organ sat, unused and gathering dust. For an instant, the minister had the impression of a person seated at the keyboard. It appeared to be a young man wearing some kind of a uniform and poised to play. But almost as soon as the preacher focused his eyes in the direction of the organ, all features of the apparition melded into formless shadows and nothing more.

Neither his faith nor his theology permitted the preacher to accept what his eyes and ears conveyed to his mind; but he had seen something, nevertheless, and became determined then and there that he would not see it again. He convinced himself that his vision was the product of fatigue and eerie conditions; and quite possibly, he had been prepared to see something by all the tales he had heard in the months since his arrival. His theological training had never directly included preparation for such encounters, but he remembered hearing older preachers warn preacher boys of Satan's ability to delude good people as well as bad.

He moved his notes and his most often-used references to a desk in the parsonage, where he did his evening studies from then on. He discovered that he worked better in the comfort of the parsonage and began spending more time at his desk there than at the church. It seemed to him that his work improved with time. He preached interesting and thoughtful sermons. The revival brought in several rededications and professions of faith. Two new families joined the congregation. The reverend's reputation had been good at previous churches, and it only improved at this one. He was an able preacher and in demand for area revivals. Because of his reputation, the church was visited every now and again by pulpit committees seeking a minister. Before the second anniversary of his arrival, he was approached by such a committee; and after a trial sermon, followed by much prayerful consideration, he was moved to answer the call.

His decision was reluctantly accepted by the church; he had made many friends with whom he kept in touch long after he left. From time to time, he was called back for homecoming, to speak at a revival, or to preach a funeral. Such occasions became separated by longer intervals with the passing of years.

After an absence of several years, he was called on to preach the funeral of his oldest friend and confidant at the church. Upon arriving, he found the church was undergoing a necessary renovation. He learned that a fire had broken out in the sanctuary, most likely from the wiring. Thankfully, somebody had seen the blaze right away and called for help. The major casualty was the old organ, which had been almost entirely consumed by the fire. Amazingly, nothing else in the building had been equally caught up in the blaze. Everything else was smelly and sooty, that's all.

The funeral was a home-going only tinged with grief. The old man had gone to be with his wife and two children. Survivors were both happy and sad at the passing. The service was kept short so there could be some visiting and catching up among the attendees afterwards. The church was once again between preachers. Attendance was up, but offerings were off; it was just the times. The church needed more youth. Otherwise, folks told the preacher, the church was pretty much like it had been when he left.

He nodded at each bit of news, shook a lot of hands, and told them he'd pray for their needs. But he did not ask about the soldier because, for some reason, the minister was pretty sure he had left, too.

THE SPIRIT OF WHITE WOLF HOLLOW

White Wolf Road turns off of South Carolina State Highway 55 about ten miles west of Clover. In contrast to the high-speed straightaway, this serene country road hearkens back to its origins in an ancient network of trails and cow paths that once led circuitously through an old country settlement, past a church site (only the cemetery of which remains), and eventually to the village that became Kings Mountain, North Carolina. Lying just outside the Kings Mountain State Park boundaries, White Wolf Road starts north and then curves back, remaining in South Carolina, before plunging down into a hollow and forking out as it emerges on the western side of the dip.

The road is the epitome of a byway, serving the interests of a handful of local residents and providing access to other highways and secondary roads that actually lead somewhere, and therefore is not much traveled. It is occasionally re-graveled when county officials feel like adding some rocks to the mud during rainy seasons.

"Modern-Day Hollow"

The hollow itself provides narrow passage for a seep that is sometimes a creek as it meanders between small hills just south of the park. At the bottom of steeply sloping, heavily wooded hills rests a simple but modern bridge that spans the creek. During the warmer months, the bridge is shaded by dense foliage. On a cool and clear autumn day, the area is aglow in vibrant colors: red, yellow, and orange hardwood leaves provide dramatic contrast to the occasional dark green of pine or cedar. However, the hollow's seclusion and tranquility belie its troubled past.

Two hundred forty years ago, a horseback ride on the roads converging toward the prominence known as Kings Mountain was anything but pleasant. The hundreds of men who made the ride in October of 1780 anticipated wounds and even death as they headed into history to fight a battle that scholars have labeled the turning point of the American Revolution.

Fighting was in its fifth year, and it was still a toss-up whether or not the goals of the Declaration of Independence would be fulfilled. Although the British had given up their objectives in the North, content to hold established positions, war raged in the South. Both France and Spain had joined the war on the side of the Americans. England could expect certain practices from its civilized opponents; but here in America, especially in the southern colonies, warfare was vicious, undisciplined. It often saw brother against brother and father against son, presaging a time in the future when America would again be torn apart by civil conflict.

In early autumn, General Lord Cornwallis was slowly moving northward from his base at Charleston and engaging as necessary the militia units commanded by South Carolina's partisan generals Marion, Sumter, and Pickens. Cornwallis' left flank was insulated from surprise by a Loyalist militia of a thousand men, commanded by Major Patrick Ferguson. The Scottish inventor of the famous breech-loading rifle bearing his name, Ferguson was the quintessential British officer. Given command, he exercised it; given a task, he did all in his power to complete it.

To suppress the American patriots in the upcountry, Ferguson served notice to the effect that, if citizens did not support the king, they would be considered in revolt and treated accordingly. He would march into their midst and "hang their leaders and lay waste to their country." Legitimate resort to arms deteriorated into depredation and terrorism. British seizure of property and summary execution of suspected rebels were met with similar retribution by the Americans.

To deal with Cornwallis and Ferguson, an assault was organized by the mountain militias in late September. Mountain men marched from Sycamore Shoals, Tennessee, across the mountains into the South Carolina upcountry. From near Hannah's Cowpens, they marched without rest through constant rain to attack Ferguson's mountaintop camp.

Ferguson's forces were composed almost entirely of American Loyalists. Some of them were high-minded men acting on principle, while others were the worst kind looking for adventure or opportunity to plunder. Ferguson assembled the largest force he could once he learned of an impending attack and retreated to the high ground on the ridge of Kings Mountain. Stragglers continued to arrive and choose sides up until the moment of engagement.

The day before the battle, on the morning of October 6, two men came upon a small cabin south of the mountain to which they were headed. The green wood cabin was new and sat in the grass above a spot where the road turned from due north to northeast. No smoke was coming from its chimney, nor was there any sign of an occupant as they got closer; the only other dwelling visible was an obviously occupied farmhouse located a few hundred yards away. Probably thinking that the cabin might contain something to eat or something of value, they entered.

Inside, a young woman was quietly gathering things she would take to her parents' house at the top of the hill, where she would stay to await the return of her husband. She had seen him off the evening before. He had left in darkness to meet with others in his local militia, which would rendezvous with those marching in from the west sometime the next day. She would be safe with her family when her husband had the opportunity to return, but she needed some things from her cabin and had to do certain chores before going back to her childhood home. It was just a short walk and should not take long.

There were no witnesses to what took place at the cabin. The young bride did not arrive at her parents' home by midday. Shortly thereafter, when she still had not come, her father went to check on her. He found the little cabin in disarray, indicating a desperate struggle. The few pieces of homemade furniture were turned over or broken; the morning's milk was spilled and drying on the rude plank flooring; the cabin door was wide open.

From the evidence, he determined that his daughter had fought for her life with at least two men, one very large and one average in size. She had probably defended herself with a butcher knife. There was blood on the cabin floor and the door. She must have cut at least one of her assailants before fleeing the cabin with them in pursuit. She had evidently run toward the creek, opposite in direction from her parents' home. The tracks in the wet sandy soil were long strides; both the pursued and pursuers had flat-out run. Evidently, his daughter had chosen to try escaping to a neighbor's cabin up the road on the other side of the hollow or hiding in the undergrowth along the banks of the creek.

Escape was not to be. Her father studied the tracks at the bottom of the hill. When the young woman had reached the tangles of vines and shrubs along the creek bank, she was slowed; there, her pursuers had overtaken her. There, she had died. The tracks of the men, bloody at first, continued up the hill. He followed them until they became impossible to distinguish on the rocky ground, but they were headed toward the mountain.

Her father returned home to break the sad news to the other members of the family. Making sure his wife was secure, he armed himself and then left with his young son to recover the body of his daughter. She was laid out and prepared by neighboring women, who dressed her in the white dress in which she had said her marriage vows. She was buried the next forenoon, most likely in the yard of a nearby Presbyterian meetinghouse or on a small rise behind her cabin; in either case, no stone or marker has survived to preserve her name or mark her gravesite.

On the afternoon of October 7, after an all-night march, a large force composed of four separate militia groups of American Patriots converged fifteen miles from Ferguson's campsite and immediately launched their attack on the Tories. The advantage was to the Patriots; the Loyalists, shooting downhill, tended to fire over the heads of the opposing force. Ferguson's men scrambled around in disarray until he decided to make a break for it, attempting to ride through the Patriot lines. After he was cut down in a fusillade of Patriot fire, the fighting diminished. Flags of surrender were held up by some of the Loyalists, but the Patriots, not being familiar with the significance of a white flag, continued firing. By the time the shooting stopped, close to half of the Loyalists were casualties, and the rest had been captured.

Surviving Loyalists were marched to Gilbert Town. Along the way, informal courts-martial were held, and nine Loyalist leaders were hanged for what the Patriots determined to be war crimes or treason. Whether or not the killers of the young bride met their fate in this fashion is not known. It was said by some that the two men were deserters from the over-mountain militia who betrayed news of the attack to Colonel Ferguson; if that is correct, their names were Chambers and Clarke. Regardless, it was never determined if the murderers had even fought in the battle or, if they had, for which side.

The young husband survived the battle unscathed. After the war ended, he moved away without justice having been done. The bride's family also left the area, it was said, for Tennessee. The abandoned cabins succumbed to the elements, and all signs of their little settlement disappeared.

It is not clear when the legend began to take shape, but it was not long after the end of the Revolution that stories of encounters with the bride's ghost began to be reported by some passing through the hollow. At local gathering places and social events, it was not uncommon for discussions to center on strange goings-on near the battlefield. A lot of people avoided the battleground itself because it was thought certain to be haunted, the place where over two hundred men had perished.

But it was the hollow to the south that was most often the site of peculiar occurrences. Many travelers reported seeing something lingering beside what was then called the South Road. Whatever it was would either vanish when one came closer or run downhill and disappear in the bushes. Those who remembered the fate of the bride concluded that the apparition was none other than the girl's restless spirit, still trying to escape her killers. Over the years, the ghost came to be called simply the "white wife," because of her appearance and the fact that her name was lost to history. The place itself was referred to as White Wife Hollow until modern times.

Three generations or more grew up before the tales of White Wife Hollow mellowed to yarns told by the fireside to entertain and frighten strangers passing through. Meanwhile, the area within Kings Mountain Township remained much as it had been when the legend took root: acres of rolling, empty countryside sparsely populated by farm families and dotted with a school, a church, a mill, and a blacksmith shop.

In the summer of 1880, Doctor Andrew Campbell, wanting to get to an injured man as soon as possible, drove his buggy the shortest way possible, which took him through the hollow. It was near evening when the doctor entered the woods at the bottom of the hill. Doctor Campbell's rig was about the best in the area and pulled by a strong young horse. They had kept up a vigorous trot much of the way, but the animal was in no way fatigued. However, when the buggy approached the bridge, the horse balked. No amount of clucking and slapping of the reins could urge the animal forward. Instead, it tried to back up, trembled, and whinnied as if sensing danger at the bridge some twenty yards away.

The doctor had never seen his horse act like this before. He applied a light whip over the horse's ears and then on its rump without result. Concerned that the skittish animal might overturn the buggy, he got out and tried to lead the horse across the bridge. It tried to rear in harness, becoming so upset that Dr. Campbell was afraid the animal would kill one or both of them.

With no other choice, he backed the animal away from the bridge, got him turned around, and went the longer way. The doctor was a man of science and a skeptic when it came to spirits, but he related the incident at the bridge to a few friends and colleagues. His story became part of general knowledge, recirculated and embellished with the retelling. As long as he practiced, patients, neighbors, and even strangers would occasionally bring it up. He claimed he never saw a ghost or anything else out of the ordinary that day. He pointed out it could have been a snake or bees or even horseflies that had spooked his horse. Having to explain his adventure soon became old, and the doctor became adamant in his refusal to say anything more on the subject.

Most of the time, people who found themselves in the hollow alone at dusk saw nothing unusual. Some travelers reported feeling uncomfortable, and others said they felt like they were being watched. Since that part of the county, especially after the 1860s, was a focal point for the manufacture of illegal whiskey, skeptics often said that the watchers were moonshiners who had stills tucked back in the brush on every creek and seep in the area. But over the years, a fair number of those who used the bridge professed to have seen something they couldn't explain – for want of a better description, an apparition. Often these apparitions were described as a misty, white glow moving along the side of the road, on the bridge itself, and on the road leading up in both directions from the bridge.

Some foot travelers reported sounds that had no easy explanation, such as crashing in the brush up the hollow from the road, as if someone were running or struggling to get through thick undergrowth. Still others claimed to have heard unearthly screams coming from the woods.

For decades, it was something of a tradition for the boys of the surrounding countryside, once they grew into their bold teens, to extend dares to their peers who lived outside the area, challenging them to go alone into the hollow at night. If and when an equally brave young man accepted the challenge, an ambush was prepared for him. He would definitely see a ghost of some sort, maybe more than one. Even the occasional adult might prank a friend by simulating the famous ghost. During the early 1970s, the hoaxes became so prolific that they masked any real manifestation of the legendary spirit.

No longer a recreation spot for the high school crowd, the hollow is quieter today. Residents living nearest the hollow have had few, if any, comments to make concerning their own experiences with the ghost. But the legend persists. Rumors and gossip continue to fuel conversation at York County's country stores, schoolhouse programs, and church meetings. Almost all of the accounts describe an encounter with a female figure attired in a long white dress, crouched in hiding or in desperate flight, head turned as if looking for a safe place to go. Invariably, when hailed or approached, the woman vanishes.

The old South Road remains unpaved today, although it is well-maintained for the little traffic it serves. It was renamed by the county many years ago, almost correctly, as White Wolf Hollow Road. But regardless of the misnomer, the well-worn stories have survived, providing a sense of mystery and excitement to a quiet corner of the county and preserving the memory of one who once sought refuge in the shady hollow and would otherwise have been forgotten.

SCRATCHER

Bowling Green is a small settlement that sits just inside South Carolina on Highway 321, about twenty-five miles west of Charlotte. Today, it is just the proverbial "wide place in the road" that motorists rarely touch their brakes for; nevertheless, the community is large enough to contain a convenience store, a post office, and its own ghosts.

There have been at least three different forms of spirit manifestations reported in this community over a span of more than eighty years, although all seem to be rooted in a single tragedy that took place during the Great Depression of the 1930s.

The structure most notable for its supernatural activity is neither ornate nor imposing in any way. It is small and sits exactly one shallow gully away from the track bed of the old railroad branch line that ran north and south through the village. As ghost houses go, it appears that it would be overcrowded if more than two spirits tried to haunt it at the same time. A modest cinder block rental house of latter days, it is not the house in which the tragedy originated; that would be over in the mill village, which was once home to a desperate man who faced losing everything.

"The House Up From the Tracks"

Bowling Green Spinning Mills began operations in 1902. It managed to remain viable despite economic turmoil, war, and foreign competition by keeping its operations small and focused on a narrow niche of the textile industry. The rising costs of cotton and the company's fiscal inability to upgrade machinery and facilities finally forced its closure in 2003. At that time, it employed about 160 workers.

In its early years, it was modeled on other textile operations, with a central plant surrounded by a modest village in which many of the workers lived. It drew its workforce from marginalized farm workers in neighboring communities who could count on the plant for a regular income, unlike farming.

During the 1920s, hard times hit the cotton textile industry on the heels of the decline of cotton farming, which was brought about by the invasion of the boll weevil and market fluctuations. Some left the mill village for good; others tried to tough it out either by going back to their family farms or by finding other work. In time, the Depression wound down, thanks to the New Deal economics of President Franklin Roosevelt, but it took the Second World War to bring the economy back to its strength of earlier times.

After World War II, prosperity returned, but not as it had been before. More and more people were able to afford automobiles and better housing than the small cottages that were closest to the mill. A few speculative houses were constructed by investors on the outskirts of the community, several at the south end of the mill property, but the anticipated evolution of Bowling Green from a little village into a flourishing town never happened.

As the older generation of mill villagers passed, a new one swept in. As often as not, the newcomers were not employees of the mill; many of them were short-term renters who worked elsewhere. The mill village grew diverse but disconnected; and, with a constant influx of new people, it slowly became a community of strangers.

Amy and Bill Stoddard and their three young children moved into one of the newer houses just off the mill property in 1967. Neither Bill nor Amy had ever worked in a textile plant before. They heard the house was vacant through Estine Dill, an old friend of Amy's mother, who lived three doors down.

Amy and Bill were having some financial issues and needed to find some sort of stability. The house was fairly new, the location was convenient, and the rent was cheap. Everything worked, and the place was clean for a rental, with no previous renters' messes to have to clean up. Paying in advance, the family moved in and lived there in relative happiness for a time. Sadly, the stress of finances had put increasing pressure on the marriage; and Bill Stoddard moved out less than six months after he and his family had moved in. It would be for just a little while, he thought. He was hopeful his moving out would allow things to settle down, and then he'd return. It turned out that Bill found things a lot more hopeful living outside marriage; and after a few weeks, he decided just to stay hopeful.

Amy, now with all the burdens of raising her kids piled on her, toed the line as much as she could, taking care of the children with just the basics and none of the conveniences of a more modern house. Bill sent some money, but it was never enough. Amy was forced to find part-time work.

Amy depended on Estine to keep the kids until she got in from work, which was always after eleven. By the time Amy got the kids into bed, she was in desperate need of rest herself but often unable to enjoy it, either being too tired to sleep or being constantly jarred awake by the clanging bell of the night train. She eventually got more or less used to her hellish schedule out of sheer determination. After a few weeks, it was not surprising that, when she finally fell into bed each night, she almost immediately dropped into a deep slumber that lasted as long as her kids allowed.

One night, after an exhausting day of heaven only knew how many hours, she climbed into bed for what was left of the night. A couple hours later, when it was still pitch black outside, she awoke with the sense that someone was in the room with her. That was not all that unusual; a visit from a child in the night was the rule. Someone inevitably had to make water or drink water or had had a bad dream or was cold or had wet the bed.

She glanced around in the darkness but saw no child. She may have been dreaming; dreams sometimes woke her up. Or Bill might have come home. Just to feel better, she mentally ran through her nightly routine. As always, she had locked the doors and thought little of any intrusion. If Bill had come in, he would have made it to the bedroom by now, so that hadn't happened. She passed that thought around a time or two and remembered that Bill also would have run into something by now if he had come in, unless he had just slumped down in the front room. Maybe one of the children had gotten a cramp or a bellyache or had needed to relieve himself.

Amy was quickly becoming more awake than she wanted to be; these days, sleep was more precious than food. Hearing some rustling, she reached for the lamp beside her bed and turned it on. Startled, she saw not her husband nor a child but an older woman, a complete stranger, standing at the foot of the bed. The woman said not a word; she just stood there, clothed in a long, black dress as if in mourning. A short veil covered her face.

Amy was still groggy and at least as surprised as she was scared. The woman seemed confused, perhaps lost. She turned her head from side to side, took a step, and appeared to be looking into the distance, searching for someone. Amy began to ask herself if this woman had wandered in off the street. Bowling Green, they said, was full of weirdos. How long she considered this could not have been more than a few seconds, but to Amy it seemed much longer; for as she watched, the older woman seemed to become aware of the lamplight and her surroundings and then to dissolve into nothing right there beside the bed.

At that point, Amy came out of the bed as rapidly and carefully as possible, forcing herself with the utmost caution toward the end of the bed where the lady had stood. She hated to pick up her feet and put them down, for fear of stepping on something dreadful. She looked around. There wasn't much room to look around in. She stepped back away from the bed and bent down to look underneath it, the chill of the room raising little bumps on her neck and arms as she raised the edge of the blanket. The woman was nowhere to be seen. Amy then noticed the floor itself; at the end of the bed where the woman had stood, there was a black circular area on the floor. It looked like a pool of freshly spilled paint. She dared not touch it with hand nor foot but watched in amazement as the black circle shrank until there was nothing left of it. Just floor.

By this time, Amy was ready to wake up; but she was already fully conscious. As her shock subsided and she began to process what she had just experienced, Amy determined that she had seen quite enough. It was not yet three in the morning, but she rushed to the back bedroom where the children were asleep and woke them. Ill and questioning, the kids were not happy to be roused from sleep.

"Hush!" Amy told them. "Somebody's got in the house. They might come back. We have to leave now."

They heard the urgency in their mother's voice and complied, cramming arms into jackets and pushing little feet into shoes. No sooner had she spoken than something bumped loudly on the back porch. With the children halfway dressed and only the necessities scooped up, Amy herded her family out the front door and into her car. It wasn't much of a car, with a broken heater and ragged seat covers, but to her it was as wonderful as a brand-new Cadillac when it coughed to life and kept moving as she missed second gear.

Amy drove to her sister's house in Clover. If she woke up more than her sister's household, it was all right; at least her family was alive. It was dawn before everyone was calm enough to listen and calm enough to tell what had happened. Sis didn't know what to make of it. Amy had been known to take a drink but didn't seem impaired at the moment. It could have been a dream, or maybe her little sister was finally losing it, what with Bill and the kids and all. Or it could all be true. Amy was blood kin, so she got the benefit of the doubt.

Amy and the kids stayed on several days. She had no plans to go back to that house, at least for no longer than it took to get the rest of her stuff. She found a rental trailer at Stones trailer park. It was a block over from her sister's and not cheap. She could deal with the mice and roaches; at least they could be gotten rid of by normal means like traps and poison. After a few days, Amy and Sis went back to the house in Bowling Green to get Amy's things. They made quick work of it, abandoning a couple of pieces of heavy furniture that they could neither lift nor haul. It was OK; the trailer had plenty of built-in cabinetry for storage.

Amy asked Estine to collect her mail if she got any and said she'd pick it up the following week. Amy felt relief knowing she would not have to go back to the house. There was a definite aura about the place – "spooky" was the best word she could think of to describe it. She didn't come right out with the details of her last night there, but she did hint enough to her former neighbor about having the living daylights scared out of her to encourage conversation.

"Well, you know about the haunted house over there in the village, don't you?" asked Estine. That is when Amy first heard the story she wished she'd known before ever coming to Bowling Green.

There had been a man, back in the 1920s or '30s, who got laid off from the mill when he least needed it. He had a wife and a baby that was just weeks old when he got word about the layoffs. They were a young couple and didn't have much of anything, including food. His fifteen dollars a week had been their only income, and it had lasted just until he received the next week's pay envelope. The young man had to find work and find it quick.

He finished wearing out his shoes walking to nearby towns and hamlets, but the answer was always something like, "I wish I could help you, but…" Some of his pals he had worked with told him he might have better luck farther away from where everybody was looking. That's when he decided to hobo.

Hoboing was not without its risks. It was not permitted by the railroads under any circumstances; if caught, a man stealing a ride might be thrown off a moving train or beaten by railroad workers. Only the most desperate individuals resorted to hoboing; but the young man had reached that point of desperation. He could keep the house for another week or two, but food was in short supply even after he got a little help from his father-in-law, who had also lost his job.

The young man rode as far as he could, scouting for work in as many places as he could cover in the time he had before grabbing a ride back to Bowling Green. He found work at Chester with a government agency, and his new employer gave him a dollar for train fare. The young man made plans to sneak a ride home and buy tickets back to Chester for himself and his wife, the baby costing nothing. He could use the rest of the dollar to purchase several days' worth of provisions for his family, likely turnips and potatoes, and they would ride in style to his new job on the earliest train he could get. He almost made it.

Somehow, in the middle of the night, he wound up on the tracks not far from the sidetrack to the mill. To avoid being caught, he decided to hang onto the undercarriage. He had done it before. He did not realize he was dozing off until he lost his grip and fell. When he hit the ground, he couldn't move fast enough to get out of the way of the massive steel wheels, which severed his left leg.

When the rest of the train had passed over him, he was still alive and not yet aware of the indescribable pain that would come; but he was beginning to bleed profusely. While he was still conscious and able to think, he dragged himself desperately toward his house, perhaps fifty yards away. How he managed to crawl one-legged from the tracks across a gully and up the slope is beyond imagination, but he finally made it onto the porch. By then, in intense pain and weak from blood loss, he had no strength to call out; he could barely make a feeble whimper. He struggled to knock on the door, but he could no longer raise himself up. He feebly pawed at the screen, bumping and scraping it until he gave out.

Inside, a young woman was tending to her baby, which was not yet able to sleep through the night. She thought she heard something like whining and scratching outside, almost imperceptible in tandem with the coos and snuffles of her infant, but she wasn't at all alarmed. Everybody who had a dog let it run loose, and it was common for the creatures to prowl at night, looking for something to eat. They were as hard-pressed to find a morsel as the people in that area were. She thought to herself, if it was looking for something to eat, it was out of luck. She was down to a cup of grits and a little flour for her household.

The next morning, she found the body of her husband, bled out on the porch. Trying to arouse attention and slowly bleeding to death, the injured man had torn off his fingernails clawing at the door.

The story of the young man's tragic end was told over and again down through the years, and it had become customary for the residents in his house to report hearing him scratch at his own door in desperation. Few people believed any of the claims, although some probably had a basis in truth; for instance, it was entirely possible that some of the inhabitants truly had heard scratching at the door, albeit by a dog. Other, much less common occurrences were more difficult to account for.

Estine wheedled Amy until Amy told her own story in detail. When Amy had finished, Estine stood there with her mouth agape. As a child, Estine had gone with her mother to pay respects at the man's funeral. The description Amy had given of the woman in black fit the dead man's mother to a T.

Amy told Estine that, if it hadn't been for the woman in her room, she would have left because of the train. The bell rattled her brain on the nights it passed, and she liked to never get back to sleep after the sound surprised her. Estine then informed Amy that trains no longer used that track; plans had been made for taking it up. Besides, if it had been a train she had heard, it would have been a horn or whistle sounding, since bells had not been used since World War II.

Amy's rental house is still there. The gully is much as it has been since the tracks were first laid close to a century ago. Where the tracks were is now nothing but a flat green path. All is in place pretty much as it was that tragic night when the man crawled out of the gully and agonizingly tried to find the help he never received. The house is in fair shape, although it has been vacant as often as it has been rented. It is the kind of place that looks good for the price at first; but no matter how reasonable the rent is, it seems high when the renter realizes he is sharing the place… and those bells…!

THE WITCHES

Witchcraft is often thought of in terms of the brewing of potions, the casting of spells, and allegiance to Satan. Historically and anthropologically, witchcraft may be understood as the belief in an individual's potential to exert supernatural forces to achieve a broad swath of objectives, either for good or for evil. Colonial South Carolina, by the beginning of the Eighteenth Century, possessed a heritage rich in the cultural artifacts of Native America, Europe, and Africa, all of which included some variant of the practice of witchcraft.

From the founding of the colony in 1670 to the present day, practitioners of witchcraft in South Carolina have passed, more or less, under the notice of officialdom. Only one significant effort to prosecute for witchcraft occurred in the colony, and that was in March, 1706, fourteen years after the execution of twenty accused witches at Salem, Massachusetts.

In Charleston, colonial Chief Justice Nicholas Trott presented his case to the grand jury for the indictment of one woman as a witch. No details of her alleged crime are known. His action came after close interrogation of the unidentified woman. She was confined to jail while a case was being built against her, eventually spending a year behind bars. In addition to having charges brought against her by civil authorities, she was further examined by Anglican missionary Reverend Francis Le Jau in early 1707. When the case finally came before a jury the following spring, the jurors declined to indict the woman.

Perhaps the unfortunate events in Salem had become too notorious throughout the colonies for a repetition of similar incidents elsewhere. Or maybe South Carolina just had too many other issues to be concerned with, including piracy, native relations, and colonial politics. These problems, along with the need for South Carolina to make money for its investors, took precedence over any questionable supernatural occurrences. Once the tumult of maintaining a viable colony had become the King's problem in 1729, any official concerns about the practice of witchcraft largely evaporated; although, as late as October 23, 1823, Tygar Baptist Church in the Dark Corner excommunicated a Brother Page for his belief in and practice of witchcraft.

A wide variety of pagan or near-pagan cultural practices, contributed by South Carolina's amalgamating society, survived in the slave quarters, Native American villages, and backcountry frontier. Many of these rituals derived from the practical development of the healing arts during a long period when very little science and a lot of guesswork went into treatment of the sick and injured. A shortage of trained physicians in the yet untamed Backcountry provided opportunity for practitioners of the arcane arts to take up the slack, especially when seasonal illnesses visited the colony. These shamans, witchdoctors, herb doctors, and midwives offered the only hope of medical care to the vast majority of an ever-growing population. By the early Eighteenth Century, one could obtain a remedy for just about any condition, ranging from gout to gangrene.

Most folk healers were just ordinary people who found or figured out effective ways to treat common ailments with the resources at hand, such as alcohol, mud, turpentine, and plants. They often accumulated recipes for easing pain, stimulating healing, or encouraging birth. They claimed no special powers or abilities, and their clients understood when things went wrong.

But there were others, albeit a minority, who claimed special knowledge or powers enabling them to go beyond ordinary healing – to restore vigor or fertility, to bring back mental balance, to concoct love potions, or even to commune with the dead. The most extreme claimed the ability to cast spells and outrageously professed evil as their credo; they remained, for the most part, isolated on the outskirts of society but were occasionally sought out for their supposed powers.

York County was reputed to be a haven for witches by the late 1700s. Shortly after peace returned to the country after the Revolution, a farmer by the name of Nathanial Rainey in the southern part of the district suddenly fell ill. His condition declined rapidly; he became progressively weaker in both body and mind. His physicians had never seen a case like it. He lost interest in his farm, his family, and his projects; nothing stimulated him to conversation. About all he could manage was to lay in bed and take minimal nourishment and sip water. The symptoms mimicked apoplexy or a stroke, but the local physicians said it was not either of these.

Rainey's family watched helplessly as he fell deeper and deeper into what appeared to be an unnatural state. No one had any idea what else to do for him. Ministerial visits seemed to have no effect upon his condition, and he was in no shape nor showed any inclination to help himself.

All conventional explanations exhausted, general opinion formed that he was under a witch's hex. The most logical suspect was a neighbor, widow Balsey Fox, who had long been rumored to be able to make her enemies suffer from a distance, but no one had ever confronted her about this theory. If it were she, no one had the faintest idea why she had done this to Rainey. Belief in her powers was so prevalent that no one dared to question her.

Rainey continued to decline until he was near death. Leading citizens in the community agreed that something drastic must be done. Their solution was based on the assumption that, if Balsey were indeed a witch, she would not admit it for fear of her own life. Both the Bible and common law provided for the execution of witches. Instead of a confrontation, the community would trick her into lifting her own curse. Under the guise of a healing service at the sick man's home, every woman in the community would be asked to utter a prayer, consisting of a comment imploring mercy with a final phrase asking for God's blessing.

Word was spread, and, on the appointed day, everyone in the community gathered but Balsey Fox. When her absence was discovered, Colonel Edward Lacey, a hero during the Revolution, volunteered to get her and bring her to the service. Lacey, who had fought in more than ten battles, feared nothing. But he was no fool, either. Balsey Fox would not be the first witch he had ever known. As a young man, he had visited a gypsy, and what she had told him had been uncannily accurate. He vowed that he would not fall into any trap Balsey might lay for him.

He swung into his saddle and galloped off the short distance to her cabin. In a few minutes, he came back with a reluctant Balsey riding behind him. Old and bent, the tiny woman had claimed infirmity and protested but had finally given in and agreed to return with the colonel. When they dismounted, Colonel Lacey's horse staggered and almost collapsed, lathered and worn as if it had raced for miles carrying an immense load. Lacy himself was slim, and Balsey Fox weighed, at most, maybe ninety pounds. The crowd of men in Rainey's yard stared in awe at the condition of the horse.

Inside, Balsey stood apart from the ladies of the community as they spoke their prayers and supplications and asked for God's blessings. Then, when it became her turn to recite the healing words that would nullify any curse she might have cast upon the dying man, she calmly and deliberately spoke in her ancient and raspy voice: "May my god bless you, Mr. Rainey."

And with that, she slipped away without notice. Only later, when it was too late, did others remember her exact words.

The second most notorious case of witchcraft in America is the fabled haunting of the Bell Witch of Tennessee. This case commands considerable interest even today because it is something of a hybrid manifestation; it began as the traditional casting of a curse by a witch upon her enemy and then continued, following her death, with the torment of her victim and his family for years until she had completed her revenge. She was believed to have been transformed into a disembodied spirit, which exhibited all the characteristics of a poltergeist and which eventually caused the death of her enemy.

John Bell and his family lived on a farm in what later became Adams, Tennessee, near the Kentucky state line. In 1817, Bell became embroiled in an argument with one of his neighbors, an older woman who made extreme threats against him because a business deal between them had failed. She died before their differences could be settled. Shortly thereafter, Bell spotted an unusual-looking animal, resembling a dog with a rabbit's head, in the field near his home. He considered it to be a freak of nature and attempted to shoot it, but he missed each time he shot. He thought no more about it until other strange events began to occur.

According to tradition, the family began to hear sounds in the night, bumping sounds as if someone were hitting the outside of the house or throwing rocks at its walls. The noises continued off and on for several months and eventually shifted to sound as if they were coming from inside the house. After another period of time, the bumping was replaced by what the family described as an indistinct mumbling, which gradually became clear and articulate enough to sing, yell, and even threaten John Bell by name. The progress of the haunting was slow enough that it was a year or more before Bell asked one of his neighbors to visit one night and listen to what they had been putting up with.

Soon the story became widely known. The spirit in the house became known as the Bell Witch and attracted considerable attention. Andrew Jackson, who was acquainted with John Bell, is said to have visited the place to learn the truth of the matter and may have heard the voice of the spirit.

Bizarre things continued to plague the Bell family for over three years. Bell weakened considerably during the progress of the haunting and died in December, 1820. A long-held tradition among avowed witches of Europe was that a witch could only practice the craft in secrecy. If anyone discovered a person was a witch, the witch would soon die. Some of Bell's neighbors believed that he had discovered his neighbor performing certain rites and thus doomed her. The haunting that followed her death was revenge for what he had done.

The witch eventually ceased to be active, but the story has lived on and remains a subject of curiosity and occasional investigation today. The Bell Witch, or her ghost, is said to remain on the property to this day, residing in a cave.

Seventy years after John Bell was supposedly cursed, a series of incidents eerily similar to the Bell Witch haunting played out over the course of a summer in Cleveland, a tiny community in northwest Greenville County.

During much of the Nineteenth Century, Cleveland was a stopping place along the state road that led from the sea to the mountains. Not too many people set out to go to Cleveland; it was just where they might happen to pause on a journey to bigger towns in Tennessee or Kentucky. In 1887, it offered postal service and supplies for area farmers; it also gained national notoriety with the sudden onset of a series of inexplicable events, including the possible demonic possession of a young woman.

For the growing season of 1887, Jesse Cleveland agreed to accept a couple named Lockaby (possibly Lockabee) as sharecroppers on a portion of his property. The Lockabys would live in a substantial, though modest, tenant house while farming some of the rich bottomland along the river, and they would keep half of the corn and cotton they produced. For the Lockabys, it seemed like a propitious find. The land was exceptional, and the terms of the agreement were fair.

The tenant house was an improved cabin to which clapboard siding had been added. Originally constructed of logs, it was small, probably with no more than a couple of rooms on the main floor and maybe a loft; but the cracks between the logs had been well-chinked, and the planking on the outside added a layer of insulation from cold and heat.

By June, the crops were growing well, and constant attention was required to keep the grass and weeds out and the soil loosened to promote growth. It was a busy time that required some of the hardest labor of the season. It was a time when the Lockabys desperately needed rest each night in order to hold out to the labors they faced during the day. It was also the time when the couple began to hear strange sounds in the middle of the night.

For a few nights, they thought little of the noise, assuming it was the customary groaning and popping of an old wooden building as it cooled off after dark. They were used to this sort of thing from the several tenant houses they had lived in before. But after a few nights, they realized there seemed to be a pattern to the sounds. The knocks sounded as if they were being made deliberately by someone or something rather than at random by expanding and contracting wood.

After several nights of disrupted sleep, the couple told Mr. Cleveland about the knocking, and he agreed to check it out and see if he could determine the cause. He invited another neighbor, Captain Absalom B. Talley, and two other men to visit the house one night to see if they could hear anything.

The men arrived after dark; shortly after their arrival, Julia Lockaby, tired from the day's work, went to bed. The men sat up with her husband. They did not have to wait long before they heard light rapping sounds coming from the wall opposite from where Mrs. Lockaby's head was resting. The sounds came in intervals, each knock getting progressively louder until they were forceful enough to rattle the house and be heard for a distance, if anyone was out there to listen. Following the knocks came a scraping sound, as if something was being dragged down the side of the wall. Rapping and sawing noises continued sporadically until about two in the morning.

The witnesses made every effort to locate the source of the sounds. They looked inside and out while the Lockabys remained inside the cabin. There were few near neighbors and no known pranksters in the community, nor would anyone in his right mind even consider pulling pranks on strangers in the middle of the busy season. The men could find no cause for the sounds and could offer no consensus on what was going on.

After that night, other manifestations developed which multiplied the Lockabys' terror. The few pieces of furniture the Lockabys owned were shifted from their original positions during the night. The tapping increased in its intensity and became almost constant some nights. Mr. Lockaby, who was more skeptical than his wife and still thought someone was just trying to scare them, could not figure out how these things were being done; Julia, however, was by then convinced the cabin was haunted and insisted they leave.

They took refuge temporarily with a neighbor who had an extra room. Within days, the knocking and rapping had migrated with the Lockabys and manifested in their neighbor's home in greater intensity than it had at their own cabin. Their neighbor evicted them posthaste. People in Cleveland became convinced that it was not the cabin but the Lockabys themselves who were haunted or possessed by evil spirits. The Lockabys had little choice in the matter: in debt to Mr. Cleveland and with their payment in the form of the excellent crops in the ground, the Lockabys returned to the nightly din of raps, knocks, scrapes, and moving furniture. But within a week of their return, it all ceased.

Around the same time the noises stopped, Julia Lockaby began to complain of strange physical sensations. She experienced pricks on her skin, like shocks induced by an electric battery. Coming on suddenly, the shocks were at times almost stunning and painful. Neither Julia nor her husband could say when or how the sensations started, but they seemed to be associated with her newly acquired ability to move massive objects with little more than a touch.

When news of these latest circumstances circulated, Julia Lockaby's condition, whatever it was, attracted scores of spectators who wanted to witness her pick up an iron plow off the ground or perform some other feat of strength to demonstrate her recently acquired powers. Described as a shy, uneducated woman, Julia only occasionally demonstrated what she could do, and then only with the greatest reluctance. Because of her naïveté and self-consciousness, she attracted interest from some serious investigators, including physicians, members of the clergy, and local professors.

Julia Lockaby's fame spread throughout Cleveland and beyond by word of mouth, and her story was eventually picked up by local newspapers. Her experience was compared with that of Lulu Hurst, an eighteen-year-old woman who, at fourteen, in her native Polk County, Georgia, had undergone experiences similar to those Julia Lockaby described. Lulu Hurst reportedly had heard knocking and rapping in her home and then found she had the ability to lift and move great weights, all of which took place after a heavy thunderstorm. In her 1897 autobiography, Hurst debunked her own purported "powers" as tricks based upon ordinary principles of physics and mechanics.

Captain Talley, in an interview with a newspaper reporter, stated that he believed Julia Lockaby was responsible for the rapping and knocking herself but did not realize it. He, unlike many of the Lockabys' neighbors, did not feel there was any element of the supernatural involved; rather, he believed the effects were produced through application of physical principles, possibly electrical energy in some way. Talley cited an unnamed witness, familiar with tricks used in shows like those of Hurst, who had tried to communicate with the force or spirit responsible and concluded it involved some sort of trickery.

Most investigators, on the other hand, considered Julia Lockaby to be ignorant and superstitious, incapable of an elaborate deception. Uneducated, she had no background that would suggest a planned deception nor any clear motive for the efforts that would be required. Her powers, whatever they were, were not showcased on a stage with props and assistants but on a tenant farm out in the country. Initially, she believed that she was possessed by spirits. She did not accept money from visitors when she demonstrated her powers. She spoke only reluctantly about her ability, which she obviously considered an affliction. Both she and her husband took the matter seriously and felt that it might lead to some more dreadful condition or possibly some spiritual consequence.

Julia Lockaby's fame was short-lived. By the fall of 1887, the novelty associated with the events at Cleveland had worn off; news coverage of the manifestations of the summer ceased. The powers of Julia Lockaby, whether they had come by possession, haunting, or some unknown natural phenomenon, had diminished if not ceased altogether.

Confusion with the career of Lulu Hurst and Hurst's imitators on the stage relegated the events at Cleveland to the curiosity shelf. Science was not yet mature enough to render a definitive verdict on the matter. Neither scholarly assessment nor proof of deception was ever obtained in the case of Julia Lockaby. That something unusual really happened at Cleveland seems well-established; precisely what and how are other matters.

THE OTHERS

There is a category of the curious that belongs right up there with ghosts and flying saucers, and that is the creatures that defy proper placement within current biological knowledge. Previously unknown species pop up all the time, but nowadays the new-to-science life forms tend to be discovered under the microscope or in the deepest trenches of the oceans. The terrestrial frontier is no more; the wilderness has shrunk; hiding places have vanished. In short, the day of finding new species of megafauna (big animals) has probably passed. Or has it?

Red was a rabbit hunter before the Second World War. His favorite hunting grounds were along the Tyger River bottoms above Greer, which are covered today by Lake John Robinson. During the 1930s, the boggy bottoms on either side of the stream grew lush and thick in the summer with tangles of muscadine, honeysuckle, and other vines. Fallen, decaying tree trunks provided shelter for rabbits, opossums, squirrels, and the occasional deer when Red and other men like him showed up in

November with guns and dogs. Red liked rabbits, especially; he liked to eat them when they'd been parboiled then baked with lots of pepper sauce and served with the light, fresh, flaky biscuits his wife, Sue, made.

Red spent as much or more time hunting as anyone. He spent many a Saturday in the thick brush, allowing his dogs to run, chase what they would, and generally work themselves into shape for hunting season. It didn't do Red too badly, either, tromping in heavy rubber boots on the wet ground. It gave him back some of the wind that a pack of Camels a day robbed from him. If anyone asked his wife where Red was, even if she didn't know for sure she would say, "The Devil Catcher."

That was how folks had designated the swamp for a hundred years or more because of its unique character. For one thing, it was the widest flood plain on the river in Greenville County. Its tangles of vines and fallen timber were legendary, and there were three hillocks that rose abruptly in conical shapes off the flat plain of the river. Two were massive, and one was much smaller. They were called then, and had been called as far back as anyone could remember, the "tater hills" because they resembled much larger versions of the storage hills that country people used to store their sweet and Irish potatoes through the winter. Some more worldly observers speculated that the hills were actually Indian mounds. Whatever their explanation, the fact remained that the area surrounding them was excellent for rabbit hunting.

As a rule, when hunting season came, Red hunted alone. He liked the peacefulness of the outdoors, enjoying sounds he didn't hear in the mill or in the village where he lived. His only hunting buddies were two mixed hounds that he transported in a homemade cage he had fastened to the bed of a peach flat belonging to the outside man at the mill. Red borrowed it from time to time in exchange for keeping it gassed up and in good shape, with the occasional rabbit thrown in.

Just weeks before Pearl Harbor, Red took his dogs to the Devil Catcher. Both he and his dogs were in fine condition for the start of the season. He parked at the end of an old cotton road on the east bank of the river and turned his dogs loose. They hit a track in two minutes, and he followed with his eyes where their baying seemed to be coming from, anticipating being uphill when the rabbit was flushed out of the underbrush.

He killed one rabbit and stuffed it in his hunting coat; then he took the dogs further into the swamp, nearer the biggest tater hill. The weather was moderate; it had been wetter a couple of weeks ago, but Red didn't figure on trouble walking his hunt. His dogs, litter brothers, were called Flake and Beau, Flake being a little bigger and more aggressive. Red could easily tell which one was where when they got separated, which they sometimes did if there was more than one rabbit involved.

Flake hit a scent about the time Red got to the riverbank, but Beau was nowhere in earshot. He was probably sniffing somewhere away from the other two. Red tried to scramble back uphill a little. Rabbits tend to run in a zigzag pattern with frequent stops unless a dog is bearing down on them. Because of their construction, rabbits are faster going uphill than dogs are, and one rabbit can usually elude one dog. Red knew that, if he was to have this rabbit, he would need to get placed for his one shot.

He got placed, saw the rabbit, fired, and missed. Flake ran up to him, but Beau didn't. Red usually called his dogs one time, and that was when it was time to quit and go home; he did this so they would get used to running and staying on the track without distraction. Since it wasn't quitting time yet, Red used his shotgun as a horn. He broke it down, pursed his lips, and blew into the right barrel. It moaned out a deep and mellow sound. Red waited five minutes. No Beau.

After fifteen minutes, Red's ears had cleared from the shotgun blast, and he thought he heard Beau whining in the distance. He started in the direction of the whining, but Flake declined to go. Try as he might, Red couldn't persuade Flake to come along. Flake just hung back, nervously shifting his feet and circling in place but not moving from his spot. Red went on alone a hundred feet or so, turned, and called his dog, but the hound just whined and would not budge, still skittish. Finally, Red went back to the dog, snapped a leash on him, and looped the end over a limb. Flake squirmed and whined as Red walked back to the hunting area.

Red used his horn again. He heard what he thought was Beau and walked toward the sound. He arrived at the base of the biggest tater hill and heard the whine coming from the hill itself. It was late in the day and hard to see, but Red could make out a hole in the side of the hill, a large hole, easily large enough for him to get in if he wanted to; but Red decided he did not want to. The whine coming from the hole sounded muffled, but any den made in a hole like that should not be very deep.

For the better part of half an hour, Red tried to coax his dog from the hole. He could not imagine why the dog did not just come on out. Red had no light other than matches and would have to rely on the moon and his familiarity with the terrain to get back. It would be bright enough; he had done it before. But right now he wished he had a flashlight to examine the hole his dog was in. He had one in the truck; but that was in the truck, not here. He wondered if the dog was lost or had somehow gotten caught.

He was about to go for the flashlight when he heard Beau growl, the most fearsome growl Red had ever heard him make. He recognized the growl as the kind of sound his dog made when confronted by another dog. But this was just a den hole in a dirt pile, right? Red heard the growling continue; Beau was definitely threatening or being threatened, but the sounds coming out of the hole were growing fainter, as if the dog were going deeper. How could that be? There were no bears or anything else around here that could hollow out a hole that big and that deep, yet here it was. He heard his dog yelp like he got hurt, then whine and whimper, each sound growing fainter or farther away, as if he were being pulled into some deeper recess within the hill. There was a final yelp and then... silence.

Red called and whistled for his dog, but no more sounds drifted back to him. He had no idea what had met up with Beau. Beau was not a little dog, either; he and Flake were half redbone hound, half beagle and well-conditioned to boot. Red heard movement in the cave and quickly dropped two shells into his shotgun and backed away. As he got back to where the ground firmed and the incline steepened toward the road, he could make out something moving at the opening of the cave. A flailing motion, it seemed, like arms obscured by the varying shades of undergrowth in the darkness.

It was just too dark to see. Red had to leave his dog apparently trapped or injured until he could come back to look for him in daylight. It was drizzling early the next morning, more mist than drops. Red skipped preaching and got back to the swamp close to noon. The sun was beginning to peep out from behind breaking clouds. Everything was pretty much like Red had left it. He started calling his dog and whistling when he got out of the truck but received no response. He took his time walking to the big hill, his hand in his pocket gripping a Colt .25 semi-automatic, just in case. He hadn't brought his shotgun; being a good Baptist, he didn't want anybody he might meet to think he hunted on Sunday. He had left Flake at the house, too.

He scoured the ground around the hill carefully. He stopped several times to listen for any faint bark or movement in the brush. There were no fresh tracks in the sandy soil nor any other sign of yesterday's hunt. Seeing no reason not to, he got down on his knees and called into the cavity for Beau, but there was no response. Red didn't get back home until late in the day, with no better idea of what had happened to his dog than he had before.

A short time later, when war broke out, Red joined the Navy and saw action in the Pacific for three years. He didn't return to the Devil Catcher until after the war. This time, he went with one of his buddies, who had four dogs. When they got to the big tater hill, the dogs paid no mind to the hole in the side of it. It was not as big as Red remembered it, and he could barely see it at first for the vegetation that had grown up around it. Clearly, nothing bigger than a fox or opossum, if anything, had been using it recently.

The men didn't have any luck at all that day. Red recalled that it had been unseasonably warm, for one thing. For a long time thereafter, the mill ran six days, and Red missed out on the rest of the season. He got out of the habit of hunting when some of the fellows at the mill formed a fishing club, and he grew to enjoy his Friday night fish supper almost as much as he had the fresh-baked rabbit. Red worked in the textile industry for the rest of his life, becoming a millwright with Daniel Construction after the cotton mill he had worked at for half a century closed down. He joined the Freemasons and later became a Shriner, these roles in addition to those of husband and father. He sometimes wondered about what had happened that day, out in the Devil Catcher; but with such a full life, he didn't let it trouble him too much.

In 1980, construction began on Lake John Robinson. When the clearing phase of the project was well underway, hundreds of acres of the old swampland were denuded of trees, vines, and brush and exposed for the first time in memory. The tater hills were cleared during a season of exceptionally dry weather, permitting modern-day explorers and treasure hunters to comb the area in search of wildlife, relics, and semiprecious stones.

Although the vast area yielded hundreds of projectile points, soapstone fragments, and other Native American artifacts, no evidence of a subterranean predator or its lair was uncovered. If there ever had been a monstrous creature inhabiting the tater hills, its existence was erased by earthmovers, logging equipment, and a manmade flood.

For the most part, zoology and ecology are sufficient to deal with reports of mysterious creatures. However, there remain lingering legitimate questions about rare but often convincing reports of encounters with indeterminate species, which some describe as "monsters." The limited knowledge we have about such entities has often been transformed from the first eyewitness accounts into myth and legend or relegated to mere hoax; but in some cases, initial reports were so credible as to give rise to a specialized, though not officially recognized, study known as cryptozoology.

In most cases, the existence of unknown creatures can be explained away as ordinary animals living outside of their usual range or behaving uncharacteristically. A few so-called monstrous entities may be the result of extreme growth or developmental aberrations in otherwise well-known species. But there are others that cannot be explained away so easily; and, until more data is available, they will continue to exist in the limbo between myth and knowledge. These are known variously by their popular sobriquets, such as Bigfoot, Champ, and Mothman.

Most of their stories are concentrated locally, tentative reasons being limited range, persnickety eating habits, long periods of dormancy, or hoaxes perpetrated on a specific segment of the public. Beast sightings are much rarer than those of apparitions or UFOs. They tend to appear sporadically, being sighted a few times by a limited number of witnesses within a relatively confined area.

The most recent exception to the rule is the Lizard Man of Scape Ore Swamp in Lee County. The first known sighting of the Lizard Man occurred in the summer of 1988, when a car was severely damaged by scratching, clawing, and possibly chewing. Vehicle owner Christopher Davis of Browntown had finished changing a tire in the wee hours of the morning when he turned to see a large creature covered with scales, which Davis later described as having reptilian features.

The thing rushed at Davis, who made it unscathed into his vehicle and drove off. The animal continued its pursuit, jumping on the car and holding on for a few hundred yards while Davis swerved from side to side trying to sling it off. It seemed to be trying to disable or tear into the car until it finally fell or jumped off.

Police investigated the incident but found no immediate evidence of such a creature. They concluded, after examination of the damage to the car and the lack of any human suspects, that the scratches and other damage were likely inflicted by one of the many bears that inhabited the area. Officers believed initially that post-traumatic stress or some similar condition may have induced a faulty memory of the experience, but the victim in this case was not the only witness to report the reptilian creature in subsequent weeks.

One report was clearly demonstrated to be a hoax, but the validity of the others could not be determined through investigation. Despite the improbability of a human-reptilian cross species of the dimensions described in the first report, public interest was ignited. Reports of the Lizard Man were published in the local and national newspapers and received national network television coverage.

As the months passed, Lizard Man sightings waned but never ceased. Reported encounters continued for years. Tourist traffic to the area increased so much and persisted so long that a public celebration of the creature was established and has been held for the last thirty years.

During the mid-1890s, it was the Varmint that terrorized the country folk of upstate South Carolina. Farmers and other residents of Spartanburg County reported loss of chickens, dogs, and other small farm animals; some were killed and eaten on the spot, while others were taken without a trace. A child reported seeing a face in the window one night unlike any face he had seen before. He could not describe it beyond saying it was "scary," and many nights of restless sleep and bad dreams followed. In the autumn of 1894, newspapers reported that the terror which had been stalking its prey near the one-horse towns of

Spartanburg County all summer had moved over into Greenville County.

Older residents recalled that this was not the first time the Varmint had raided local settlements. It had a history of similar attacks going back several years. There would be a rash of stock killings over a span of several weeks, and then it would all stop as abruptly as it had started. Maybe five, six, or seven years would lapse, and the pattern of unexplained livestock killing would happen again. It was always ascribed to the Varmint.

No one could say what the Varmint was; no one could reliably describe it. Attempts to trap it, track it, or hunt whatever it was all failed. It managed to avoid baited traps and elude farm dogs. The farmers and their hands agreed that they did not have the skills of their ancestors, whose lives often depended on hunting.

The Varmint was just as dependable and just as unpredictable as the weather. It seemed to make its rounds on a grand scale that required years to complete. Its return was usually marked by the late-night sound of its distinctive howls or screeches. Speculation that it was a mountain lion or a wolf didn't seem to make sense; their calls were clearly distinct from each other, but the Varmint's noises were something else entirely. Neither did its feeding habits add up; the prey was so diverse that it could only be surmised that the Varmint was some kind of carnivore. Whatever it was, it didn't eat beans.

The Varmint was believed to have been sighted a few times, but the sightings were from a great distance, which made it difficult to estimate the animal's size and conformation. Its tracks were said to be unusual, but they were often indistinct. Several community-wide hunts were organized on the theory that, if enough men with guns were in the field at one time, they could scare up something to shoot at; but the hunts never produced the desired results. Imaginations ran rampant, with folks considering every possibility from exotic species to demons.

A loose-knit hunters' association had been organized in Greenville County during the early 1890s. The group, composed of a handful of mostly businessmen and professionals, was organized by a man named Cox, who imported red foxes from the north and released them on farmland in the upper county to be hunted for sport. It was a small, private association of which the public was not generally aware. When the existence of the group became generally known, it aroused the ire of a number of farmers, especially those who had recently lost chickens and turkeys.

The farmers blamed the imported foxes for their losses and no longer the legendary Varmint. They publicly demanded the hunters cease and desist in importation of foxes, fearing the foxes would overrun the county and decimate flocks. Neither event happened; the hunters kept the fox population under control and even assisted in looking for the Varmint after the mystery animal abruptly moved into Greenville County and started killing sheep near Highland. Whatever it was, it apparently left no scent that trained hunting dogs were interested in. Some of the dog handlers attributed the lack of tracking success to dry weather, which was known to hamper dogs in their ability to pick up and stay on scent. The dogs sniffed around the blood and remains of the slain animals and seemed to pick up a trail but then just stopped, returning to try again but never able to stay on track.

Telegrams of inquiry were sent to Asheville and Rutherfordton officials, describing the depredations and asking if wolves from the mountains would be a reasonable hypothesis. Officials from both towns replied that no wolves had been seen in their vicinity in fifty years.

A lull in the Varmint's activities came in September and through early October. Then, during the last week in October, the Varmint struck the barns or chicken houses of three farmers on Buncombe Road in Greenville County, killing or maiming twenty full-grown chickens and a calf. W. F. Thackston found some tracks and saw what he thought was a big white dog around midnight. He waited up to try to get a shot at the animal, but it stayed at a distance out of range for his gun. Examination of the tracks suggested a large dog, but to attack a yearling calf weighing well as much as a man was out of the question for any dog known to Thackston or his associates.

After the October incidents, the matter became a problem for the county sheriff. Perry Gilreath was highly respected for the abilities and insight he brought to the office. With eighteen years' experience and a reputation as a fearless lawman who did not carry a firearm, he excited public confidence when he formed a search with bloodhounds to find the Varmint. Following scents left at the freshest kill sites, the sheriff and his officers pursued the Varmint for two days and nights in the woods; however, their search was without results.

Then, almost predictably, the slaughter stopped as suddenly as it had in the past. The end of the stock losses raised as many questions as the beginning of them had. What had happened to the creature responsible? Some thought that it had died from poisoned bait put out by some of the farmers, but no one claimed to have killed it, nor did anyone produce a carcass. Others thought it had simply moved on, but there were no subsequent reports from anywhere in the surrounding area of any similar occurrences. Whatever the reason, the Varmint did not trouble the farmers of Greenville County any further.

About 1928, incidents similar to those involving the Varmint occurred north of the Bethany-Santiago community in western York County. During the late summer, several residents noticed losses of chickens, goats, and other livestock. Hogs and cattle were unmolested but for one. The weather had been wet enough that tracks had been left, but they did not match those of any animal known locally. No one saw anything; all of the harm was done at night, mostly in silence. Unlike the Varmint, the creature responsible took its prey one at a time; that is, when one farm experienced a single loss, that was it for the night. This was apparently the feeding pattern of some wild animal. The question remained: what animal?

The oddest act of this mysterious beast was that it attacked a residence. A man who worked for a mineral company in North Carolina was awakened by his wife just after midnight one August night. She had heard noises outside and concluded that someone was trying to break in. The man whipped his cover off and grabbed for his pants and shotgun. He was as quiet as he could be, but as he got fully awakened and organized, he realized he had heard nothing yet.

He was about ready to go back to bed and dismiss the event as a dream of his wife's when he heard the noises himself. It sounded like somebody walking on the roof and then clawing at it. All the man had for illumination was an oil lantern, and whatever was out there would be above him, so he decided to wait and see what happened next. He looked out the windows, hoping to see a shadow of his visitor cast by the light of the moon. It was a clear night, but he saw no shadow. All became quiet as he and his wife sat on the edge of the bed listening intently. After a long while, he declared that whatever it was had gone and suggested they get some sleep.

A couple of hours later, the clawing began again in earnest, very fast, like something trying to dig into the roof. The wife didn't have to wake her husband the second time; he was out of bed and on his feet when the racket started. The house they lived in was roofed with shake-shingles, made out of wood and single-nailed in place. He was afraid that whatever was clawing would actually dislodge some of the shakes and get into the cabin. He later said that he visualized a catamount trying to tear into the cabin. He grabbed up his shotgun and ran out the door, firing one barrel in the air. He then turned and, aiming over the chimney to avoid shooting his roof, fired the other barrel before rushing back in and slamming the door and reloading. He had no idea whether his shot had struck anything, and he didn't see anything during his brief foray into the yard.

Whatever it was, that was the last anyone heard of it in the community. Residents concluded that it must have been a panther instead of a wildcat. No one in the area had ever seen one, but they all had heard stories; there was also some historical record available. When the naturalist John J. Audubon was in the state in the fall of 1831, he estimated the average weight of the Carolina panther at about the same as an adult man. Standing three feet at the shoulder, the panther was certainly large enough to bring down a human and, as the species was being hunted into extinction, some may have been bold enough to begin stalking humans. By 1860, the Carolina panther was no longer found throughout most of the state. The few surviving animals were believed to be relegated to the great swamps of the Lowcountry.

Could the Varmint and the creature of York County have been two of the few remaining Carolina panthers, prowling outside their usual haunts? Or was there something unnatural terrorizing the farming communities of the Upstate? Just as backcountry dwellers at the time could not know for sure, neither can we.

During the late 1950s, excitement again swept over the Upstate after local newspapers detailed discovery of the lair of what came to be known as the "Devil Beast." For three years, since 1956, residents along Highway 25 north of Travelers Rest had been aware of some strange creature's presence in the woods and fields. This "something" had farmers in the area going to their fields each day expectant and armed. It was rarely seen and then only from a distance or obscured by brush. When humans encountered it, the creature showed little fear and took its time moving back into cover.

The animal in question had been killing chickens, turkeys, some domestic pets, and other small livestock. Losses had been increasing, prompting area farmers to compare notes. Several reported encountering a strange predator during the last several months. Whatever it was could be heard howling in the night; it made sounds unlike that of any other animal native to the area. Heard early in the pre-dawn hours, its cry was similar to a shrill human scream. The animal was described variously by men who saw it. M. L. Loftis, a tenant farmer, described it as large, brown, and furry, with white horizontal stripes and weighing sixty to seventy pounds. John T. Hopkins, who believed he had located the den of the creature, noted the size as similar to that of a Great Dane; tracks left by the beast were larger than a man's hand, making it in the area of perhaps forty inches tall at the shoulder and weighing anywhere from a hundred to a hundred eighty pounds.

Much speculation had been put forth as to what the creature was. Some who had not seen it suggested it could be a bear or even a large dog. Eyewitnesses said there was no mistaking it for a bear. They also ruled out any large cats, including bobcats, pumas, or mountain lions. Hopkins believed that the one he saw was a female and that it had cubs. That would imply a mate and perhaps more of the creatures in the area. The beast(s) seemed to range over the area from Travelers Rest to the Marydell section and around Tigerville.

After the story broke in the local newspapers, hundreds of would-be Devil Beast hunters descended on the area. Within days of the first reports, Hopkins tallied over two hundred cars passing his house before two o'clock in the afternoon when, on an average weekday, only the mailman and one or two other vehicles might come by.

Most of the visitors were armed men, bringing with them everything from deer rifles and shotguns of various gauges to a red jeep that Hopkins claimed sported a tripod-mounted machine gun fully loaded with a belt of ammo. An off-duty FBI agent reportedly showed up at the scene with his own hunting dogs just out of curiosity, as the incident did not fall under federal jurisdiction. Some residents had already tried to use hunting dogs to track down the beast, but the dogs shied away from its scent. The one dog present with Hopkins when he saw the Beast was cowed badly and ran back to the farmhouse.

As public interest abounded, so did the number of reports of encounters with the animal. One man reported that he had gone to get water from a spring when the Devil Beast sprang from the brush and attacked him before he was able to raise his gun. Unable to fire, he beat off the attack with the butt of his gun and made his escape by climbing a tree and remaining there until the animal left. Another farmer was said to have lost twenty-eight turkeys without a trace of evidence of what happened to them.

The sheriff's department increased patrols on the roads of the northern county as the frequency of reports increased. Many parents in the area did not permit their children to have the usual summer freedom. Despite the best efforts of farmers and the interested public, the beast proved elusive. There was no shortage of opinions as to what was really out there, some people suggesting species that were far beyond the realm of possibility, like Tasmanian wolves and hyenas. Grasping for answers, speculators could think of no other candidates to put forth but those that were usually found far from the Carolina Backcountry.

Sightings slacked off towards the end of that summer, but the few that were reported increased the range of the animal. One creature about the size of a small bear was reported near the Greenville Reservoir. The beast was believed to have moved downslope in July to the Blue Ridge area, where it was captured by a cattleman and his dogs. The captured animal was determined to be a longhaired wild goat with an impressive set of horns. Three weeks later, a new sighting of the Devil Beast was reported to the Greer Police Department, the creature having been spotted near town on the grassy edge of the Southern Railroad tracks. It was said to have attacked dogs in the city.

By the last of August, sightings in the highlands of the county had diminished to almost none. One of the last reports came from a resident of Locust Hill, who saw a large bobcat clearly immobilized in the headlights of his car. The motorist observed that the bobcat's features matched many of the Beast's identity markers, as cited by others, and concluded that it was probably the animal responsible for all the excitement. Few agreed with him.

That fall, some photos of animals were shown to individuals who may have seen the Devil Beast; all animals were native to the North American continent but some were creatures rarely seen in the southeast. One of the closest matches turned out to be a coyote, except that its size and behavior did not fit. About the same time, some rethinking about the behavior of the Beast led to the possibility that it was a wild boar, strayed from the mountains. Feral hogs were abundant in certain parts of the highlands, and they had been known to kill chickens and dogs. They were even known to have attacked and injured horses. Their markings were extremely variable and could include stripes, and they were at home in the woods and fields. The problem with the wild hog hypothesis was that these animals made a different sound from that ascribed to the Devil Beast; they also left plenty of wallowed-out depressions in the ground, none of which had been found.

Questions remained which still cannot be answered. Some of the facts of the case of the Devil Beast are remarkably similar to the temporary appearance and behavior of other unidentified creatures described in South Carolina folklore. In most instances, the encounters were brief, descriptions varied, and law officers and knowledgeable people were unfortunately absent when the beasts made their appearances.

If it is so that there indeed are strange, undiscovered species of relatively large build still out there, one thing is certain: as the state fills with humanity, whatever is in the remaining wild areas will be pressed into either extinction or relocation. If it is the latter, then there remains opportunity for some members of the public to experience the joy of discovering firsthand and face-to-face some previously unknown element of the natural world.

IMPORTED MONSTERS

During the Eighteenth Century, American ports were flooded by tens of thousands of Scots-Irish and other United Kingdom immigrants, a large number of whom eventually settled in the Southern Appalachians, which were not unlike the topography of the immigrants' homeland. When they came to the New World, they brought with them their recipes for whiskey, their knowledge of seafaring, and their taste for tea. They also brought their songs, poems, and legends to be passed down to ensuing generations. One such legend describes a human monster who possessed the worst characteristics of a predatory creature.

Seaney (or Sawney) Bean was said to have been born on the coast of Scotland during the reign of Elizabeth I. He ran away from home as a child and learned to fend for himself early, mostly by stealing. Since theft was a capital offence in Sixteenth Century England, Bean became adept at covering his tracks and evading the law. He managed to survive by his wits and physical prowess to adulthood, when his behavior further deteriorated. Without moral or religious instruction to guide him, he thought nothing of committing murder to gain what he wanted or to cover up his crimes. He hunted the Queen's deer and stole livestock belonging to villagers. He held up and killed travelers. He abducted women for his own dark pleasure, one of whom he forced to become his wife. He brought her to his favorite hiding place, said to be a cave near the sea.

Together, in a strange bond of love and depravity, they raised a family that eventually fell even farther below any human standard. Somehow, perhaps during an extended time of famine or for the novelty of the practice, Bean and his family acquired a taste for human flesh. During their heyday, they robbed, killed, and evidently devoured dozens of victims. According to tradition, when their cave hideout was eventually discovered by authorities, it was littered with human as well as animal bones, both sets showing evidence of butchering.

Before the extent of the Beans' activities were fully known, reports of missing travelers or townspeople were considered by authorities as individual incidents rather than a single, strung out case of mass murder. Highwaymen were blamed; but while many were hunted down, tried, and hanged, the disappearances neither ceased nor declined.

Years passed, and the depredations of the Bean family remained obscured amidst the generally lawless climate of the early Stuart period of English history. Eventually, however, a slip-up was made. Maybe it was Bean's increasingly frequent raids to support his growing family that stimulated more diligent searching by the authorities. Whatever the cause, the king's soldiers tracked them down and captured most of the family. By this time, the eldest children had followed in their parents' footsteps. After brief trials, Seaney Bean, his wife, and the children old enough to be held accountable for their actions were hanged. Younger children may have escaped or been rescued. It is just possible that one or more Bean children grew to relatively normal adulthood and sired a family. Possibly, descendants of Seaney Bean made it to America.

Three hundred years later, give or take, a story very similar to that of Seaney Bean emerged from the Carolina mountains. The story, which began as a campfire tale and has undergone transformation into several versions, describes the abnormal development of a boy who emigrated from Europe with his parents about 1900. The Rudy Randover tale echoes some of the most horrifying elements of the Seaney Bean legend, while its details have been Americanized, localized, and updated by each successive generation.

From an early age, Rudy Randover exhibited disturbing, violent inclinations. He grew rapidly to an unusual size and possessed great strength by the time he was an adolescent. His uncontrollable behavior forced his parents to move from town to country, eventually settling in upper Greenville County.

Perhaps they thought a rural environment would have a calming effect on the boy, but that was not the case. In the age before serial killers and mass murderers became commonplace, he demonstrated perverse and cruel behavior, torturing and killing pets and the domestic animals of neighbors. For a time, his father was only able to restrain him by chaining him at night with heavy shackles anchored to the wooden floor.

He would not, could not be held; with his maturing strength, Rudy worked at his irons until he freed himself. He then ripped the chain from the floor and escaped into the woods, where he lived by his cunning. It is said that he returned home one more time to kill his father before becoming the monster people talked of but never saw. Livestock was stolen, killed, and sometimes partially consumed. Sometimes it seemed to have been ritually consumed, with only the eyes having been eaten, for example.

Stock in the Backcountry had free range until roundup time in the fall, and farmers of the area had always accepted the fact that there would be losses to various predators, like bears and wolves, and even some rustling by their neighbors. When more than a few animals began to disappear and half-eaten carcasses began to show up in the high meadows, people grew concerned. The old folk had heard of things like this before; not that they knew for sure what was going on, but there was no telling what kind of creatures lived back up in the high mountains.

Reports of missing travelers had also long been a part of the mountain experience, but most of them simply turned up late or at the wrong place, usually a little worse for the wear of having been lost, hurt, or subject to exposure. A few did die, especially when alcohol was involved, but their bodies were almost always found. When a couple of people disappeared completely and remained gone without a trace, hunts were organized for the bear or wolf that was responsible. The hunting parties had no luck tracking it down; it, whatever it was, figured out ways to elude the best dogs and the best trackers around. Only the discovery of some oversized footprints led to the suspicion that the "monster" responsible was human, but he was clearly both deranged and exceptionally clever.

Once it was established that the subject of the search was a man, officers of the law were called in, and the search party became a posse. With ample personnel and plenty of motivation, the posse soon found, near River Falls, a rock shelter that had been used as a den. The man-monster was not there, but it was undoubtedly his lair; it was littered with bones and fragments of what appeared to be animal carcasses, and the smell was fresh if not appealing.

Two deputies were posted to remain close and keep watch for the outlaw; they were to arrest Randover and bring him to Greenville when he returned to his den. The officers assigned to this duty were temporary deputies. Often called "dollar deputies," these lawmen were ordinary citizens who either volunteered or were commandeered to help in hunting down distillers of illegal whiskey. These particular deputies were mountain men known to be able to handle the roughest class of moonshiners.

After several days, with no one having been brought in, a regular deputy was sent out to see how things were going. He reported that the two lawmen had disappeared and that there was no sign the occupant of the cave had returned. At the time, no one thought much about it; irregular officers were known to quit a job if something better came up or they got homesick. No new depredations had occurred, and locals began to think the wanted man had probably left the vicinity. The situation was much discussed for a while and then forgotten, as all things eventually are. Only much later was a leg bone found that probably, at one time, had helped to prop up the taller of the dollar deputies.

Rumors then abounded that the bad man was back. The sheriff asked the state's help, and the militia was deployed to the mountains under the general supervision of the sheriff. How long this combined force beat the bushes is not known. Reports of casualties came in as if the fugitive were somehow managing to take deliberate revenge against those who were trying to capture him. Different accounts came down the mountains each day the search was in progress. Rumors picked up to fill in the gaps where factual details were absent, and superstition took its part in painting the big picture. Some came to believe the killer up there was more than a man, that he could not be caught, could not be killed.

In time, the enthusiasm of posse members waned as their numbers fell off. The militia had to return to other duties. Official records of these events are missing from the files, and, as far as is known, there was never an arrest made in connection with this case.

With the passage of time, the facts of the situation were obscured by dramatic license in the retelling. John Pete Taylor, a longtime Scoutmaster from Greer, was famous for reeling off ghost stories for hours on end during the 1950s and 1960s. At Camp Old Indian, he often told the story of a half-man, half-beast who still lived in the Carolina mountains. Taylor had heard the story in his youth and found that it worked well to quell the spirit of misbehavior and mischief in the boys he led.

"They'd wet their britches before they would leave their tent after dark," he once explained. The story remained popular for decades and apparently made its way to every resort or youth camp that could scrounge up enough firewood to create the right atmosphere. It was so popular at Camp Greenville that the Greenville Piedmont ran a feature on it.

The connection between the stories of Seaney Bean and Rudy Randover is conjectural but likely, considering the numerous similarities between the two. It is probable that both narratives were fueled by actual events; but their longevity is not based in fact but in legend. Legends are more powerful when they are separated from the present by a span of time, even if that span of time would logically preclude the monster's continued existence. Still, if there was any truth to the legends of a superhuman monster of a man lurking in the backwoods at one time, perhaps such a man could still live in some form.

LOST GOLD

Few stories excite the imagination as much as those of buried treasure. The idea that life-changing riches lie within reach for the bold and determined is enough to prompt anyone to pick up a shovel. The Carolina Backcountry has had its share of wealthy individuals who may have squirreled away a small fortune for leaner times; and modern-day treasure hunters labor in hopes of finding such a cache nestled in a wall cavity or secreted under a barn floor. According to the tales that follow, these hunters may not be laboring in vain.

During the American Revolution, South Carolina lands and waters saw more battles and skirmishes than any other state. The Battle of Cowpens was one of two battles which took place on South Carolina soil within a three-month period and which were pivotal in turning the tide of the war in favor of the Patriots. It was fought on January 17, 1781, pitting British Colonel Banastre Tarleton against Brigadier General Daniel Morgan.

Using tactics still studied today by military students and historians, Morgan overwhelmingly defeated the opposing force and narrowly missed capturing Tarleton, who managed to escape the field with a handful of men. For his actions, Morgan was one of only seven participants in the Revolution to receive a Congressional Gold Medal.

After Morgan's death, the medal could not be found and was feared to be lost to history; a replacement was created early in the Nineteenth Century. In 1972, Mack Evans was trying out a metal detector along "an old Indian trail" near Greer. There, he unearthed a medal, all but hidden in the remains of a leather pouch, which strongly resembled the one awarded to Morgan in 1790. It had somehow been separated from its original owner and buried, either by natural forces or by human hands, until its discovery nearly two centuries after the battle.

In midwinter, 1935, on the bank of Hard Labor Creek in McCormick County, the old home place of the Dorn family was consumed by fire. The house had been built by William B. "Billy" Dorn after he struck it rich almost in his own backyard.

Billy Dorn was born in 1799 and had modest holdings in 1835 when, according to one account, a traveler noticed some colorful rocks on Dorn's property and brought them to the attention of the owner. Dorn, a cotton planter, turned from agriculture to mining after the discovery, but capitalizing on it proved elusive. He prospected and test-mined for years before he found hints of ore near a neighbor's property. Dorn began commercial mining in 1852 and, within a year and a half, recovered three hundred thousand dollars' worth of gold from a three-hundred-foot section of a vein of ore.

Dorn built the finest house in the area, with ten rooms in two stories. Shortly thereafter, the fifty-six-year-old bachelor courted and married Mattie Rutledge, age fourteen. He continued to operate his mine, but the returns diminished as the ore bodies were exhausted and no new ones found. Mining operations ended during the Civil War and did not resume afterwards under Billy Dorn's name.

While he had money, Dorn was something of a philanthropist, donating land and funding public works. During the war, much of Dorn's gold supported the Confederacy. Shortages of draft animals and disruption of the cotton market and transportation contributed to his farm falling into ruin. In 1865, when scouts from Sherman's army reached Dorn's plantation, they found barren fields and empty barns; a few slaves were filling up a gully near the sawmill with rocks. Being that the place was already so depleted from the impact of war, the scouts passed by without molesting it.

Dorn never again lived the comparatively flamboyant lifestyle he once enjoyed, nor did his plantation return to anything like it once was. Conditions in the state were bleak for years after the end of the war; shortages of manpower and capital resulted in pockets of the extremely destitute, both black and white. Dorn struggled along like his neighbors for years, trying to make crops with his sons and to hold on to the land. His sons grew up in poverty, but the oldest, John C. Dorn, said that his father always promised that he would take care of the family. John understood his father's words to imply that there was yet some resource they could fall back on. Four years later, Billy sold his mine, reportedly for twenty thousand dollars, to the inventor of the mechanical reaper, Cyrus McCormick, for whom the town and county were later named. There were, by then, debts and taxes to catch up on, and the expenses of maintaining the farm consumed Dorn's seeming windfall.

Billy Dorn died unexpectedly of a stroke near the end of Reconstruction but still long before the state even began to recover from the war. By the late 1870s, he had run through all his apparent wealth and supposedly died in poverty. Talk in Hibler Township, though, was that old Billy Dorn had not died poor: he had held back a reserve of gold for himself. Speculation was that Dorn had secretly buried the last of his gold in an iron chest at the bottom of the gully. Once it was covered in dirt, he had had his slaves pile rocks in the ditch to secure his treasure until a later, safer time. Once the danger of loss was gone, Dorn may have retrieved his treasure and reburied it in a more secure spot and simply waited on destiny to catch up with him.

This chest of gold was never found. The younger Dorn believed the chest was real, but his father had never told him where it was hidden. The story of the treasure was eventually dismissed by locals because of Dorn's marginal financial condition at the time of his death. But his family apparently did not suffer. His sons married successfully, became independent farmers, and remained near their childhood home; his widow moved to Gainesville, Georgia, and ran a hotel. The family seemed to have an easier time than most in war-torn South Carolina, which raises a few questions. But then, consider the eccentricities of a man who became the richest man in the state by taking unusual chances. What are the odds that he didn't put away something only to lose it in the end?

John Carman came from Tennessee sometime after 1815 and settled with his family about seven miles north of Greer on the banks of Beaverdam Creek. He was a blacksmith by trade and ran a small gristmill as well. When the War Between the States came, Carman served in the Confederate army doing general blacksmithing and making Bowie-style fighting knives. Afterwards, he returned to his work as a blacksmith, and his business thrived in the years after the war. Carman taught his trade to his sons and took on apprentices at a time when skilled metal work, although hard labor, was much more certain than farming, which was the predominant occupation in the state. He expanded his smithy to include building and repairing wagons and carriages; he also extended himself to other types of work, investing in real estate on a short-term basis and later becoming a trial justice. He led a successful life until an accident ended his days of work in the 1880s.

Carman suffered a fractured skull as the result of being struck by a piece of a grindstone that disintegrated at high speed in his mill. The injury produced pressure on the brain which, in turn, caused a gradual personality change and other symptoms that worsened with time. There was nothing local physicians could do except wait and observe; the kind of surgery that might help was still in its infancy in the 1880s.

During his decline, Carman's fortune, mostly in gold coins, disappeared. His wife revealed that he had previously hidden his money in the bottom of an old well bucket, which he kept filled with lighter wood beside the kitchen stove. She didn't realize the bucket was gone until her husband's condition had deteriorated to the point that he could no longer communicate reliably. No one had any idea when the bucket had disappeared; it had been, as any piece of furniture in the house, ordinary and unnoticeable. The family theorized that Carman had hidden the bucket himself.

One of his grandchildren claimed that he saw his grandpa carrying the bucket down a hill toward a small creek that ran through the pasture south of the home site and on into his brother's place. That had been weeks, if not a couple of months, earlier. Carman was still ambulatory in the late stages of his condition and required careful watching to prevent him from harming himself or others. Things became so difficult that he was eventually taken to the lunatic asylum in Columbia, where he could be given what was deemed proper care.

He died there in 1885, memory gone, unable to carry on any conversation. The administrators of his estate were unable to recover many of his papers and records and none of his money. He had apparently destroyed or hidden his documents and most likely hidden his wealth, since he had not traveled from his home nor engaged in business transactions since the accident. During the interim period between the accident and his transfer to Columbia, he had freely wandered about his farm while he was able, occasionally doing purposeful work and behaving normally. He died having written no will; there was no clue as to the precise amount of money he had possessed at the time of the bucket's disappearance. Attempts to discover his hiding place proved futile.

He was survived by three sons, who initially spent time digging as often as their regular work would allow, but they held out no false hopes. The curious noted that John Carman's fortune was never spent; questions were raised and rumors eventually spread far and wide beyond family conversation, to the extent that outsiders visited the property from time to time, uninvited and at odd hours, digging in likely spots for the missing treasure. The size of the treasure grew in the public imagination to a well bucket full of gold, then two buckets full, which would have been impossibly heavy even for a young man in robust health, much less for an elderly and injured man, to carry any distance. At a time when cotton prices were in slow decline, few diggers questioned the rumors and scheduled their excavations for the wee hours of moonlit nights.

This clandestine treasure hunting persisted for years, dying down when no one apparently found the gold and then returning, with the onset of the Depression and the loss of jobs and income, as a nighttime activity for the Carman descendants to endure. Family members living in the old house during the 1930s reported that they would go to bed at night only to wake up with new holes and new piles of dirt hither and yon over the property.

Interest again waned with the onset of war and this time did not return, as the excitement of a hypothetical buried treasure paled in comparison to the real prosperity and optimism of the 1950s. In time, the children of John Carman died out, and the next generation lost interest altogether in their lost inheritance. The property passed into other hands, the old house became a rental property, and the house and outbuildings aged into ruin.

Of John Carman's family, none died rich. No latter-day generation of Carmans nor their allied families was ever known to experience undue prosperity. Most of the descendants by the third or fourth generation either were unaware of the treasure or believed that, if there had been one, it had long ago been excavated in secret. Who knew? It could be that the strongbox had been purloined while Grandpa yet lived and was himself unable to protect it.

Still, there remained a spark of hope in the memory of certain distant cousins and non-kinsmen who had long memories. One of the last surviving grandnephews believed that there were only two places that had not been scoured for the treasure. He discussed these possibilities with his own nephews (he never married) not long before he died. He said that the most sacred place to the old man was the gravesite of his son Benjamin, which was located near the front of the house and surrounded by crape myrtle bushes that had grown tall. The grave had never been molested. A simple stone marked the resting place of one of twin boys born in 1857; the other boy had lived to a ripe old age. If that was not the hiding place, then it was likely near the springhead that fed the creek at the end of the pasture. It was near Uncle Mike's cabin, Mike being John's youngest son. The family always called the trickle Mike's Creek. For John Carman, it had been his quiet place. It had been his habit to go out in the woods to have his personal devotions, to think, and to be alone as necessary. It is certainly possible that, as his mind grew more and more disquieted, John Carman put his most valuable possessions in one of the places that brought him the most peace.

FORGOTTEN TREASURES

In order to be lost, a treasure first has to be found. In South Carolina, the Spanish arrived during the early Sixteenth Century with that specific objective in mind. Their mission was twofold: subdue and evangelize the heathen; and discover and seize the wealth of unclaimed lands for Spain. With these goals in mind, conquistadores organized expeditions into the interior regions of Central and South America, Mexico, and the North American southwest and east coast, from what would become Florida into North Carolina. Four Spanish expeditions moved across parts of South Carolina. The earliest Spanish visit was a brief landing at the mouth of the Santee River in 1521. This was followed by an attempt at colonization along the coast by Vasquez de Ayllon in 1526, which was abandoned after his death.

The first dedicated expedition into the Carolinas was led by Hernando de Soto. De Soto had landed in Florida in 1539 under orders to explore and colonize the lands north of Florida. De Soto proceeded northward, probably arriving near Silver Bluff in the Savannah River Valley in March of 1540. From that point, in search of gold, he traveled northeast across South Carolina to the Native American chiefdom of Cofitachequi, located near present-day Camden on the Wateree River. Cofitachequi was rumored to have a great treasure, but it turned out that the treasure was in the form of freshwater pearls, which were surrendered to the Spanish by the female chieftain, or cacique. Gold, according to the natives, was located further upcountry. De Soto's trek continued northward and westward in a haphazard pattern into the mountains to find it.

The route taken by de Soto has long been the subject of debate among scholars. Accounts of the journey by some of de Soto's companions often proved confusing until recent decades, when newly discovered archeological evidence was used to supplement the journals and memoirs left by actual participants. The most current thinking is that de Soto's main body crossed the Savannah south of Little River and marched through the middle of South Carolina to a point near Camden before turning northward. In the mountains of western North Carolina, without having discovered significant treasures, the de Soto expedition continued westward, eventually reaching the Mississippi River, where de Soto became ill and died. At that point, his expedition, having been over three years in the field and reduced to half strength, collapsed into a trek for survival.

There were two major problems that de Soto had not foreseen. The first was that his expedition did not carry adequate rations and so found itself heavily dependent upon the indigenous peoples' supplies of corn. This limited the expedition to an itinerary that led from village to village rather than directly to the best leads for gold. A second problem was that the natives of the southeast did not value gold as highly nor in the same way as did the Spanish, to the point of being unable to identify the mineral accurately. Weather, numerous necessary water crossings, and the hostility of some tribes also shaped the fate of the expedition, which ended with the death of de Soto in 1542, after which the survivors turned south toward the coast and returned to Florida.

De Soto was also just plain unlucky. On his way to a grave in the Mississippi River, he passed very close to four fabulous goldfields that were later mined commercially, millions of dollars' worth of the precious metal being extracted from them. The first site was the Dorn deposit, located in McCormick County within about forty miles of where the Spanish crossed the Savannah into South Carolina. This deposit was discovered and mined extensively during the 1850s. Two other locations were on either side of de Soto's path: to the east was the Haile deposit in Lancaster County, which was discovered in 1827; to the west were the goldfields of latter-day southwestern York County. After leaving North Carolina and Tennessee, de Soto passed tantalizingly close to the deposits in northern Georgia, which were discovered in 1828 when the land still belonged to the Cherokee. The deposits there were rumored to be so rich that the natives named the place Dahlonega, meaning "yellow stone" or "gold," for the nuggets that could be found on the surface.

Some old legends of Spanish presence in the Savannah River Valley and nearby outlying areas do not precisely jibe with the latest interpretation of the evidence. Stories describe a Spanish mining operation near the Savannah River, ostensibly continued by a small party of men until they were wiped out by a hostile tribe. The legends have persisted since the era of the American Revolution and stimulated attempts to locate and mine old Spanish diggings.

Whether it was de Soto's expedition or a later one led by Juan Pardo that provided the spark of inspiration that ignited the legends is unclear. The current thinking about the route of march of both de Soto's and Pardo's expeditions puts the Spanish well over a hundred miles east of where the legends of Spanish gold and silver were persistently sought; however, de Soto was known to have sent out scouting parties from his main force. Some contingents of de Soto's force may have covered a much broader swath of ground as the search took the main body of the expedition into Cherokee territory. It is possible that a handful of deserters or stragglers saw evidence of precious metals near the original location of the Old Rock Church in what became the Abbeville District. If legend contains truth, the area was first mined by the Spanish and later hidden by the Cherokee to prevent encroachment on their hunting grounds by an influx of settlers. According to tradition, it was during that time that the Cherokee may have been mining silver and cinnabar for ornamentation and ceremonial devices.

Two decades after de Soto's journey, Juan Pardo led two expeditions, the first in December of 1566 and a second in September of 1567. Scholars believe Pardo followed in de Soto's footsteps at least to the center of the state and thence northward, where some mineral wealth was discovered. But a twenty-pound piece of archeological evidence exists which puts Pardo or some of his men around present-day Inman sometime in 1567, a location well off the route established by recent scholarship.

The curious relic – perhaps placed to measure a distance or to stake a claim or to mark some feature of the land – was discovered by a farmer in 1934. Bryson Hammett, while plowing his field, unearthed the roughly rectangular rock, which bears the date of 1567 along with other symbols of indeterminate meaning. Because of the date, the stone was linked to the Pardo expeditions; it was examined and later authenticated by historian David D. Wallace. Whether further excavations were made for other related relics on the property is not known. The stone itself is now part of the collection in the Spartanburg Regional Museum.

Accounting for the Inman relic being well off the route now accepted for Pardo's journey remains a problem. Pardo went on to establish several small forts as far inland as present-day Morganton, North Carolina, where it is believed some smelting activity was carried on. Pardo left one relatively large garrison at a village near the present-day town of Marion under a commander named Moyano, while Pardo himself continued to advance in the tracks of de Soto; it was almost a year before he saw Moyano again.

Meanwhile, according to records, Moyano ventured as far as four days' travel from his post to maintain a Spanish presence among the area chiefdoms and to prospect for precious minerals. Moyano was keenly interested in discovering precious stones or metals within his sphere of duty. He managed to find deposits of unidentified crystals at three or more sites by the time Pardo returned, but they did not prove to be of great interest. Pardo was concerned, by then, for the safety of the expedition and its return to Santa Elena. As with the de Soto expedition, finding adequate supplies of conveniently located corn or other foodstuffs was always a priority.

As he made his way back to the South Carolina coast, Pardo left behind small forts garrisoned by small numbers of men. The intent was obviously to return and continue to develop a route from Santa Elena, located on present-day Parris Island, to the mines in Mexico, although the route would have been unnecessarily circuitous. The natives, however, had no incentive to respect the Spanish presence when the main body of soldiers was gone and wiped out the tiny advance guard Pardo had left in place. The garrisons' fate was probably never known by Pardo, who, for whatever reason, sailed back to Spain and did not return to the Americas.

A century later, English traders no doubt picked up information about hidden stores of precious metals while they conducted the more mundane business of the deerskin trade. Tales of a lost silver mine on Coronaca Creek were circulated among the troops sent to quell the Cherokees during the Indian War of 1760. No doubt most who heard the stories dismissed them as prattle heard around the evening fires. No further record of any attempt to find and open the mine before 1800 is known. The vast and fertile lands of the Backcountry beckoned to practical men who craved the opportunities that came with the free parcels awarded to veterans of the Revolution. Self-sufficiency and personal independence took precedence over digging holes on prospect.

During the early Nineteenth Century, a small group of investors sank a shaft at the supposed location of the Spanish mine and worked for some weeks. Nothing of value was found at the site. The precise location of a mineshaft had supposedly been determined by the use of a divining rod, but it did not, apparently, pan out. About the same time, on the banks of Bush River, hand-worked silver ornaments were discovered among common stone relics of the Native Americans who had inhabited the area previously. The silver source could not be determined with any degree of certainty, since peace between tribes produced considerable potential for trade over the hundreds of miles of paths connecting them; but the old legends gained credibility, nevertheless.

The lost silver mines of western South Carolina either have remained lost or were so privately and secretly operated that they never became known except in legend. Without firm grounding in regional geology or the requisite technology to carry out a systematic exploration, prospectors and investors of the Nineteenth Century had to rely on hit-or-miss methods to find what treasures could be found. Visual inspection combined with placer mining and careful study of landforms sometimes led to the right decision about where to dig. Just before the Civil War, it was reported that silver was being mined farther north in the Pickens District. The ore body was located at a depth of fifteen to thirty feet. This location would have been in Cherokee territory a century earlier and perhaps fits in with the earlier legends.

One of the earliest discoveries of gold in the state was in the Greenville District about 1802; gold was eventually found in eighteen South Carolina counties in both lode and placer deposits. Three of the locales contained gold in commercial quantities. It may seem surprising that these discoveries did not lead to a Carolina gold rush to rival that of California or the Yukon; but an important fact to remember is the low value of gold in 1800 relative to its value today. At the time of the initial discovery, cotton was the real "gold" in the Upstate because, in the fertile fields of the foothills, it was a certainty rather than a risk. Still, gold was a resource that could be sold for a profit, which led several men of property to invest in mining operations.

James H. Randolph, an upcountry cotton planter, discovered gold on property about eight miles north of Bailey's Crossroads and partnered with neighbors David and John Mosteller to buy a parcel of land northeast of Mosteller's Mill in September of 1833. The description of Randolph's discovery suggests he found a lode deposit (a primary or main source) but apparently did not know enough to put much time and energy into mining it. It was evidently enough to interest him but not enough to devote the full-time labors of his slaves.

Randolph apparently lost what interest he had and negotiated a complex swap with Lemuel Loftis in 1834, in which Randolph agreed to exchange the land for a slave and a horse and pay boot to retain the right to work the land a little longer. That deal fell through, but Randolph was able to sell the property the next year to a newcomer named Vardry McBee of North Carolina. McBee worked the placer deposit downstream with cheap white labor and limited slave labor until the beginning of the War Between the States. McBee had better luck than did Randolph, the diggings producing close to a hundred thousand dollars' worth of gold, which he sold to the United States Mint.

McBee gave interest in the gold mine to his daughter, Martha, and son-in-law, Tench Carson, in 1843. The mine became known thereafter as the Carson McBee mine. Carson died in 1861, three years before his father-in-law; when McBee died, even though the mine had produced almost five thousand ounces, he reportedly had only explored a small part of the bottomland where the ore had been discovered. Up to that time, practically all of the gold that had been extracted had been taken from gravel beds that had washed over eroded quartz veins. The gold content in these "stringers" was exceptionally rich, amounting to between ten and thirty-two dollars' worth of gold per ton of ore. The placer mine was said to be in decline by the time of McBee's death, but it is unclear whether the known veins had been exhausted or the lack of manpower had put the operation on hold. Another possibility is a lack of available funds in the war-ruined South to support continued mining. Whatever the situation, McBee Bottoms remained unworked for many years afterwards.

It took decades for the South to develop local investment capital, and what local funding was accumulated was almost invariably put into the rising cotton manufacturing business. The mine languished for another quarter-century. Expansion of the operation might lead to new unexploited veins, but the risk was great. Only after the first New South cotton mills became profitable did even small amounts of capital become available for mineral exploration in the Upstate, and it was never to finance major and systematic exploration of McBee Bottoms and the surrounding countryside.

Yet, the Bottoms were never completely forgotten. A few intrepid if dream-inspired gold hunters prospected and panned the property off and on for years, sometimes with permission and sometimes unauthorized. A few would-be prospectors made public announcements of reopening the mine, perhaps hoping at the same time to attract investment capital for better mining technology. They based their pitch on the twin facts that extractive methods of the early Nineteenth Century were crude and that McBee had not completely explored what he had.

Spartan Dickson – inventor, farmer, and businessman – was given permission to explore and reported finding a vein of gold-bearing quartz on the McBee property in late 1887. Some dismissed his claim as exaggeration, as his enthusiasm was somewhat excessive. Whatever the reasons, Dickson was unable to convince anyone to partner with him on the venture. The following spring, prospector Thomas Farmer reported finding a large nugget, which he showed to potential investors. Despite receiving no investment capital, he set diggers to work shortly afterwards; however, a few weeks of systematic excavation produced no find of any significance, and Farmer left the project. The mine lay abandoned for twenty years.

In 1910, E. H. Mason made public his discovery of gold nuggets at or near McBee Bottoms, but the section that looked most promising was being farmed. Weighing the potential profits from cotton and gold against each other, the landowner(s) chose cotton. The land was not further developed as a mining property.

Frank Rogers, an Alaskan prospector, leased a considerable area in the vicinity in 1927 and sought investors. He claimed to have found nuggets the size of birdshot, but he did not produce enough of them to attract the kind of investment he needed. The lively stock market on the brink of Depression attracted whatever investment capital was available.

During the early days of the Great Depression, some small operations were resumed at McBee Bottoms; but in 1933, President Franklin D. Roosevelt issued Executive Order 6102, forbidding ownership or hoarding of any but a minimal amount of gold. The same year, the price of gold was fixed at thirty-five dollars an ounce, raising its value overnight from around twenty dollars; but between the federal penalties of ten years in prison or ten thousand dollars in fines for hoarding and the slate of regulations for operating a federally approved mining operation, further interest in McBee Bottoms was deterred.

Again, decades elapsed before interest in local mining perked up. Gold ownership by United States citizens was again permitted in 1975 when the official government price was a little over forty dollars an ounce. Once again, a little interest was generated in the McBee site and other upcountry locales that looked promising. In 1991, the McBee mine was again prospected for a short while without any known success. The project collapsed when one of the partners died the next year, and no other serious attempt to excavate the site has since been undertaken.

Packs Mountain is a small, rounded, and once-forested prominence in Highland Township that was determined to contain gold-bearing rock by about 1880. Small amounts of alluvial gold were first discovered in the gravels of Wildcat Creek, which carried sediment from the mountain. Exploration uphill from the creek led to the opening of a mining operation by Manley Bright in late 1884. The gold he found was negligible, but that did not deter others. Attempts to extract gold from Packs Mountain continued off and on for another forty years. At least three shafts were excavated in pursuit of gold-bearing quartz veins; another was built to extract other associated minerals. The amount of precious minerals found, however, proved too small for the investment required, and the mines were abandoned by the 1920s.

During the 1960s, Dr. J. Roy Jackson, a Greer dentist and amateur prospector, examined ore from Packs Mountain and noted its similarity to the ores located at Smyrna, South Carolina, which had produced commercial quantities of gold dating from the turn of the century. Despite interest and occasional prospecting, the Packs Mountain mines were never developed beyond exploratory shafts and the use of minimal technology.

If indeed the ore from Packs Mountain was of the same quality as that of Smyrna, the early prospectors may have done well to continue their search. Smyrna is a modest, secluded town in the southwestern part of York County; but belying its humble appearance, the area around and including Smyrna's Martin Mine has produced the most extraordinary examples of South Carolina gold.

The Martin Mine is one of forty-eight historic gold mines in York County. They are all geologically related to each other and to the massive body of rock that underlies the region going northward into Mecklenburg County, North Carolina, where one of the first gold rushes in American history began.

Martin Mine was initially worked during the 1830s. The geology is not unlike that of McBee Bottoms. It was developed from a placer deposit but later worked by open pit and shaft mining technology. It produced the largest amount of gold from this type of deposit of any mine in the state. A single specimen of mixed gold and quartz weighing twenty-seven pounds was discovered fifty or more years after mining operations had begun.

Mining technology and the price of gold have both improved drastically since operations ceased at the mine. The surrounding land was allowed to grow up in trees, which were later cleared for the pulpwood. By the 1960s, the mine had been reclaimed by nature. However, nearby diggings on a smaller scale continued quietly during the 1970s. A family living in the area in 1973 mined gold so successfully that they were able to produce at least a few round ingots of about a quarter-ounce. They had to do their work in secret, however, as the law at the time still prohibited individual ownership of that much gold; possessing bullion as they did was not allowed until January 1, 1975.

Despite wildly fluctuating gold prices since 1975, only cursory interest has been paid to the Smyrna goldfields. The main obstacle to large commercial mining in this region is the fact that most of the deposits are small. The rich gravel bed at the Martin Mine was only about a hundred eighty thousand square feet in area. Nevertheless, the potential for small fortunes to be made with modest operations still abounds in York County.

South Carolina, even today, ranks among the top states for gold production, but the masses of ore required to extract one ounce of bullion are enormous. Gold may be found anywhere in the northwest corner of the state, but the greatest potential for discovery seems to lie on the blades and point of an arrow-shaped region which runs from the counties of York to Oconee and back to Greenwood. Many of those early sites where gold was plentiful have likely never been explored adequately nor completely, either because of limitations in the technology at the time or a lack of necessary investment. These are the most favorable sites, which might still yield fortunes, with ore bodies at rest under the soils that once grew cotton and now sport housing developments.

The Backcountry of South Carolina still holds some potential for modern-day prospectors. Many interesting crystals and some semi-precious stones are spread across the Upstate. Rock hounds of the Palmetto State have found fine crystals of clear and smoky quartz in the Greer area, as well as massive examples on the slopes of Paris Mountain within the boundaries of the state park; amethyst has been found in several locations around Anderson County; garnet, black tourmaline, and limonite crystals have been found in Spartanburg County just inside the county line near the village of Apalache; and angle-plated quartz has been found near Travelers Rest and at the summit of Packs Mountain.

There are other forms of treasure remaining to be found in the Carolina soil, probably less valuable intrinsically than historically but still fascinating nonetheless. For all treasure hunters and would-be seekers of fortune, the key word is respect. Ask permission before hunting and do no damage while searching. Good luck and good fortune!

Also by Ray Belcher

*Greenville County, South Carolina:
From Cotton Fields to Textile Center of the World*

With Joada Hiatt

*Greer: From Cotton Town to Industrial Center
Greer: Then and Now
Legendary Locals of Greer*

INDEX

Abbeville District, SC, 178
Apalache, 82, 188

Bailey's Crossroads, 181
Bell Witch, 133, 134, 135
Bell, John, 133, 134, 135
Bigfoot, 148
Blue Ridge, 157
Bowling Green Spinning Mills, 120
Bowling Green, SC, 119, 121, 123, 125, 126
Bright, Manley, 185
Brother Page, 130
Bush River, 5, 6, 7, 11, 12, 13
Bynum, Turner, 34, 36, 37, 38

Camden, SC, 8, 176
Camp Greenville, 164
Campobello, SC, 53
Carman Family, 171, 172, 173, 174
Carson, Martha, 182
Carson, Tench, 182

Champ, 148
Charleston, SC, 18, 80, 111, 129
Cherokee Nation, 177, 178, 180, 181
Chicago, 80, 83
Civil War, 1, 35, 69, 169, 171, 181, 182
Cleveland Community, 135, 137, 138, 139, 140
Cleveland, Jesse, 135, 136, 137
Clover, SC, 109, 124
Cofitachequi, 175, 176
Colvin, Broughton, 85, 87, 88
Confederacy, 105, 169, 171
Cowpens, SC, 112, 167

Dahlonega, GA, 177
Dark Corner, 47, 53, 54, 130
Davis, Christopher, 148
de Soto, Hernando, 175, 176, 177, 178, 179

Devil Beast, 155, 156, 157, 158
Devil Catcher, 142, 143, 146
Dickson, Spartan, 183
Dodson, Dorothy, 81, 83
Donaldson Air Base, 97
Dorn, John C., 169, 170
Dorn, William, 168, 169, 170
Dover Family, 57
Dover, Gat, 71
Draper, Lyman C., 12
Dutch Fork, 5

Evans, Mack, 168

Farmer, J. M., 49
Florida, 175, 177
Flynn, W. L., 82
Fox, Balsey, 132, 133

Gainesville, GA, 170
Galbraith, Henry, 6, 10, 11
Gilbert Town, 114
Gilreath, Sheriff Perry, 152
Glassy Mountain, 47, 48, 54
Great Depression, 119, 121, 158, 173, 184

Greenville County, 83, 87, 135, 142, 150, 151, 152, 161, 181
Greenville, SC, 1, 4, 25, 31, 36, 37, 77, 163
Greenville Mountaineer, 36
Greenville Reservoir, 157
Greenwood, SC, 187
Greer, SC, 81, 83, 84, 141, 164, 168, 171, 185, 187
Greer Police Department, 157
Gullick, Judge M. L., 50

Haile Gold Mine, 177
Hammett, Bryson, 178
Hard Labor Creek, SC, 168
Hatton's Ford, 36
Hayes, Ed, 47, 48, 49, 50, 51, 52, 53, 55
Hendersonville Road, 53
Hibler Township, 170
Highland Township, 48, 50, 151, 185
Hopkins, John T., 155, 156
Hurst, Lulu, 196

Inman, SC, 178, 179

Jackson, President Andrew, 196
Jackson, Dr. J. Roy, 185

Kings Mountain 109, 110, 112, 115

Lacey, Colonel Edward, 132
Lake John Robinson, 141, 147
Lancaster County, SC, 177
Le Jau, Reverend Francis, 130
Lee County, SC, 148
Lindsay, Dr. J. H., 49
Little River, 176
Lizard Man, 148, 149
Lockaby Family, 135, 136, 137, 139
Lockaby, Julia, 136, 138, 139
Loftis, Lemuel, 182
Loftis, M. L., 155

Mahaffey, S. O., 82, 86
Marydell Community, 156
Mason, E. H., 184
Mattie Rutledge, 169

McBee, Vardry, 37, 182, 183
McBee's Bottoms, 183, 184, 185, 186
McCormick County, SC, 168, 177
McCormick, Cyrus, 170
McKinney, John, 48, 49, 50
Miles, Charity, 5, 6, 7, 8, 9, 10, 11, 12, 13
Miles, David, 5, 6, 7, 8, 9, 10, 12
Miles, David, Jr., 5, 6, 7, 8
Miller Road, 89, 93, 95
Miller, John, 33
Mississippi River, 176, 177
Moore, Chief Dave, 81, 82, 83
Morgan, General Daniel, 167, 168
Morganton, NC, 179
Mosteller, David, 182
Mosteller, John, 182
Mothman, 148
Motlow Church, 39, 43
Moyano, 179

Native Americans, 130, 147, 175, 176, 177, 179, 180

Nell's Woods, 32
New Deal, 121
Nullification, 36, 38

O'Neill's Mill, 5, 9
Oconee County, SC, 187
Old Rock Church, 178
Old Stone Church, 33, 38

Packs Mountain, 185, 186, 188
Pardo, Juan, 177, 178, 179
Parris Island, 179
Patriots, 6, 33, 111, 114, 167
Pendleton, SC, 33
Perry, Benjamin F., 36, 37
Pickens District, SC, 33, 181
Pickens, Andrew, 33, 111

Rainey, Nathaniel, 131, 132, 133
Randolph, James H., 181, 182
Reconstruction, 170
Revolutionary War, 5, 12, 33, 35, 111, 115, 131, 132, 167, 168, 177, 180

Roaring Twenties, 80
Roosevelt, President Franklin D., 121, 184
Rudy Randover, 161, 163, 164

Salem, MA, 129, 130
Saluda Gap, 25
Savannah River, 175, 176, 177
Scape Ore Swamp, 148
Seaney Bean, 159, 160, 161, 164
sharecropping, 39, 57, 135
Sherman's army, 169
slavery, 18, 19, 20, 21, 26, 27, 29, 30, 31, 70, 72, 130, 169, 170, 182
Smyrna, SC, 185, 186, 187
Spartanburg County, 83, 87, 149, 150, 179, 187
Suddeth, James, 50, 51, 52, 53

Talley, Captain Absalom B., 136, 138, 139
Tapp, W. J., 82, 83, 84, 85, 86, 87, 88

Tarleton, Colonel Banastre, 167, 168
Taylor, John Pete, 164
Tennessee, 112, 115, 133, 135, 171, 177
Thackston, W. F., 152
Thurston, William, 25, 26, 29
Thurston's Hill, 26, 27, 30, 31
Tigerville, SC, 156
Tories, 7, 8, 114
Travelers Rest, SC, 25, 155, 156, 188
Trott, Chief Justice Nicholas, 129
Tygar (Tiger) Baptist Church, 130

Varmint, 149, 150, 151, 152, 153, 154

Wallace, David Duncan, 178
War Between the States, 1, 35, 69, 169, 171, 181, 182
Wateree River, 176
Watson, Adam, 85

White Horse Road, 25, 31
White Wolf Road, 109, 118
Wildcat Creek, 185
Wilson, John Lyde, 35

York County, 118, 131, 153, 154, 177, 186, 187

www.ingramcontent.com/pod-product-compliance
Lightning Source LLC
Chambersburg PA
CBHW072001290426
44109CB00018B/2097